THE EUROPEANISATION OF INDUSTRIAL RELATIONS

The German-English translation has been produced by Lionel Fulton and Richard Pond, Labour Research Department, London; technically assisted by Henning Schmincke, University of Bremen

The Europeanisation of Industrial Relations

National and European processes in Germany, UK, Italy and France

WILHELM EBERWEIN
JOCHEN THOLEN
JOACHIM SCHUSTER

LONDON AND NEW YORK

First published 2002 by Ashgate Publishing

Reissued 2018 by Routledge
2 Park Square, Milton Park, Abingdon, Oxon OX14 4RN
711 Third Avenue, New York, NY 10017, USA

Routledge is an imprint of the Taylor & Francis Group, an informa business

Copyright © Wilhelm Eberwein, Jochen Tholen and Joachim Schuster 2002

The authors have asserted their moral right under the Copyright, Designs and Patents Act, 1988, to be identified as the authors of this work.

All rights reserved. No part of this book may be reprinted or reproduced or utilised in any form or by any electronic, mechanical, or other means, now known or hereafter invented, including photocopying and recording, or in any information storage or retrieval system, without permission in writing from the publishers.

Notice:
Product or corporate names may be trademarks or registered trademarks, and are used only for identification and explanation without intent to infringe.

Publisher's Note
The publisher has gone to great lengths to ensure the quality of this reprint but points out that some imperfections in the original copies may be apparent.

Disclaimer
The publisher has made every effort to trace copyright holders and welcomes correspondence from those they have been unable to contact.

A Library of Congress record exists under LC control number: 2001098450

ISBN 13: 978-1-138-72740-3 (hbk)
ISBN 13: 978-1-138-72733-5 (pbk)
ISBN 13: 978-1-315-19086-0 (ebk)

Contents

List of Figures and Tables   *vi*

Authors   *vii*

List of Abbreviations   *viii*

1. Introduction: A comparative study on the development of industrial relations in Germany, France, Great Britain and Italy   1

2. The process of Europeanisation and the development of industrial relations - theories   13

3. Selected empirical findings on the development of industrial relations in Europe – current research   24

4. Views from trade unions and employers' associations experts - National and European experiences   36

5. Relations between national and European levels of industrial relations - five case studies   81

6. Future prospects - Developing industrial relations in Europe as a contradictory process between national and European regulation   157

Bibliography   *166*

Index   *172*

List of Figures and Tables

Figure 5.1   The EWC and its interaction partners   83

Figure 5.2   Zanussi: Consultation and controlling committees
             (Company Level)   106

Table 1.1   Industrial relations in Germany, France, Great Britain
             and Italy   12

Table 5.1   Electrolux in Europe: Production units and largest
             warehouses respective distribution facilities (1998)   102

Table 5.2   Zeneca's EWC representatives   145

Table 5.3   Composition of the EWC AstraZeneca   151

Authors

Dr. Wilhelm Eberwein and Dr. Jochen Tholen, University of Bremen (Germany), senior researchers, co-ordinators of the project 'Europeanisation of Industrial Relations'

Dr. Joachim Schuster, University of Bremen (Germany), researcher, currently member of the state's parliament of Bremen

List of Abbreviations

AEEU	Amalgamated Engineering Electrical Union
AEG	Allgemeine Elektrizitäs-Gesellschaft
AG	Aktiengesellschaft / Public Company
BR	(German) Works Council / Betriebsrat
CE	comitè d' établissement / (French) works council
CEE	(Countries of) Central and Eastern Europe
CEEP	Centre Européen des Entreprises Publiques / Central European Association of Economy
CEO	Chief Executive Officer
CFDT	Confédération Française Démocratique du Travail / (French) Democratic Worker's Confederation
CGC	Confédération Générale des Cadres / (French) General Confederation of Employees
CGIL	Confederazione Generale Italiana del Lavoro / General Association of Italian Workers
CGT	Confédération Générale du Travail / (French) General Confederation of Work
CGT-FO	Confédération Générale du Travail - Force Ouvrière / (French) General Confederation of Labour - Workers Power
CHF	Swiss Francs
COBAS	Comitati di base / base committee
DEC	Digital Equipment Corporation
ECB	European Central Bank
EEF	Engineering Employers Federation
EFBWW	European Federation of Building and Woodworkers
EIRO	European Industrial Relations Observatory (based in Dublin)
EMF	Europäischer Metallgewerkschaftsbund / European Metalworkers Federation
EMCEF	European Mine, Chemical and Energy Workers' Federation
EMU	European Monetary Union
ETUC	European Trade Union Confederation

ETUI	European Trade Union Institute
EU	European Union
EURO	Single European Currency
EWC	European Works Council
FIEC	Federation of the European Construction Industry
FIET	Fédération Internationale des Employés, Techniciens et Cadres / International Association of white collar Employees
FIM	Federazione Italiana Lavoratori Metalmeccanici / (Italian) Association of Metal Workers
FIOM	Federazione Impiegati Operai Metalmeccanici / (Italian) Association of Metal Workers
GBR	Gesamtbetriebsrat / Joint Works Council (in accordance with the German law)
GMB	General Workers' Union
GmbH	Gesellschaft mit beschränkter Haftung / Public Limited Company (in accordance with the German law)
GPMU	Graphical, Paper & Media Union
GWC	General Works Council (in accordance with the German law)
HBV	Gewerkschaft Handel, Banken und Versicherungen / (German) Union for Trade, Banking, and Assurances
IG	Industriegewerkschaft / (German) Industrial Trade Union
IG BAU	Industriegewerkschaft Bauen, Agrar & Umwelt / (German) Industrial Union for the Building Industry, Agricultural Industry, and Environment
IG BCE	Industriegewerkschaft Bergbau, Chemie & Energie / (German) Industrial Union for the Mining Industry, the Chemicals Industry and Energy
IG Metall	Industriegewerkschaft Metall
IRES	Institut de Recherches Economiques et Sociales / (French) Institute Economic and Social Research Institute, Paris
LO	Landsorganisationen / Land Organisation / Union Association (Sweden)
LRD	Labour Research Department, London
NGG	Gewerkschaft Nahrung, Genuß, Gaststätten / German Food Industry Trade Union
RSU	rappresentanza sindacali unitarie / (Italian) United Union workplace union
SE	European Public Company (coming from the French abbreviation)
SME	Small and Medium-sized Enterprises

SMIC	Salaire minimum interprofessionel de croissance / Minimum Wage (France)
SMUV	Schweizerischer Metall-und Uhrenarbeiterverband / Swiss Metal and Clock Worker's Association
SNB	Special Negotiating Body (to set up EWC)
TGWU	Transport and General Workers' Union
TUC	Trades Union Congress
UCATT	Union of Construction, Allied Trades and Technicians
UILM	Unione Italiana Lavoratori Metalmeccanici / (Italian) Union of Metal Workers
UK	United Kingdom
USA	United States of America
UNICE	Union des Confédérations de l'Industrie et des Employeurs d'Europe / (French) Union of Industrial and Employer Associations of Europe
UNIFI	Finance Industry Union
VEBA	Vereinigte Elektrizitäts-und Bergwerks-Aktiengesellschaft
VIAG	Vereinigte Industrie-Unternehmungen
VW	Volkswagen
WC	Works Council
WEM	Western European Metal Trade Employers Organisation

1. Introduction: A comparative study on the development of industrial relations in Germany, France, Great Britain and Italy

The concept of the study

Although the economic integration of the European Union is far-advanced, its social dimension remains underdeveloped. This is particularly so in industrial relations where far-reaching economic developments are leading to major changes. For example, the establishing of the European Monetary Union may have lasting effects on industrial relations. As long as there is no effective co-ordination of national economic policies, collective bargaining policy and industrial relations will take on a special importance as the participating countries adapt to the different economic developments.

The implementation of the EU directive on European Works Councils in September 1996 provided a new impetus to the potential Europeanisation of industrial relations. But it is still early days and a whole host of questions remain to be answered.

Whatever future developments emerge, employees are going to be affected - directly or indirectly - positively as well as negatively. Often there is considerable uncertainty about and lack of information on the economic, social and legal situation of employees in the other EU countries; whether there is a "Europeanisation" of industrial relations at all; and what is the potential for co-operation and co-determination of worker representation in the plant and from the trade unions etc.

These and further questions were the reason for conducting a study on the development of industrial relations in selected countries, to be able to identify the different national trends as well as the possible interaction between national and European levels. For this purpose, we interpret Europeanisation of industrial relations as a socio-political process, that is: it is based on representation of different interests and therefore requires political regulation - and it is also socially based, and therefore presenting a specific interrelation of inter-action.

Industrial relations in Germany are used as a point of reference against which selected aspects of industrial relations in France, Great Britain and Italy are compared and contrasted. Industrial relations in these four core EU countries vary in specific ways and provide plenty of opportunity to compare and contrast the different systems.

Our general interpretation of the term industrial relations in the first instance is that it covers:

- economic exchange processes;
- the social relationships and conflict between capital and labour; and
- the contracts, norms and institutions issuing from these social relationships.

Specific areas of study include:

- workplace and company organisation;
- collective bargaining;
- trade unions and employers' associations; and
- government regulations and legislative standardisation.

The main focus of the study lies in the changes within the plant and the company. Collective bargaining, employers' associations and legislative regulations are considered, but only in so far as they are of importance at plant and company levels. In addition, placing the main emphasis on different aspects, we concentrated on the five differently structured sectors of industry - the metal industry, chemicals, food, construction, trade and insurance. By having this spread of industries we can highlight the potential features specific to each but also reach more general conclusions.

The fundamental approach of the project revolves around the concept of a process of Europeanisation, which is by no means clearly defined. In the political as well as with the technical discussion, there were conflicting interpretations:

Does the Europeanisation of the working community and the interaction between the national and European levels of industrial relations lead to a conformity of industrial relations in the individual countries of the European Union (convergence)?

Or, do the national models remain more or less untouched by the developments already mentioned (divergence)?

Or, do industrial relations in the European Union develop into a complex interrelation of international and supranational arrangements, which differ fundamentally from the traditional united state as well as also from standard supranational regulations?

For each of these assumed paths of development, there are theoretical and empirical arguments which confirm as well as refute them. It is not our intention to go into these at this point. At the present time the Europeanisation of industrial relations seems to us to be a process whose form and outcome remain to be determined and within which respectively standardising, exaggerated, yet opposing development trends are possible:

1. According to the intensity of the standardisation, the development process of labour relations will follow a course between harmonisation (alignment) and heterogenisation (differentiation).
2. According to the degree of legislative standardisation, the Europeanisation of industrial relations will be influenced by the partly contradictory processes of regulation as well as de-regulation.
3. According to the form of the dialogue and the way in which the conflict is dealt with, the Europeanisation of industrial relations will swing between the conflict model and co-operation model.
4. Finally, the Europeanisation of industrial relations with respect to the relationship of company and worker representation in the area of conflict of single-structured (for instance, in Great Britain) and dual-structured (company and worker representation as for example in Germany) forms of representation will have to be relocated.

Against this background, the project pursued several objectives: it consisted of an investigation of a rapidly developing subject area which will be extremely important in the future and which highlights a whole host of questions and problems.

At the same time, the project explicitly aimed to provide a practical service in publishing this report as well as having an educational function for worker representatives at plant and union levels.

Many conferences were held bringing together representatives from companies and associations along with technical experts not only for the purpose of gathering information, but above all to stimulate the political discussion about involvement and co-determination by employees in the European unification process.

It was also intended that the planned project would enable the increasingly dynamic process of the Europeanisation of industrial relations to be integrated into continuous project work and to demonstrate suitable possibilities for how this could be structured.

The aim was to take into account the requirements of an exchange of employee-orientated research especially as a result of bringing appropriate, practising researchers together with company and union worker representatives.

The project was carried out by dividing the work into several steps:

1. Evaluation of empirical studies already carried out and a review of relevant literature;
2. Talks between experts, unions, works councils, representatives from employers' associations or trade associations as well from management;
3. Case studies in the parent companies and subsidiaries of combines in the different countries and sectors of industry;
4. National and international conferences and workshops on specially chosen topics, involving unions, employers' associations, companies and workplaces, to guarantee a continuous feed-back amongst the people involved; and
5. The establishing of a working group "European Works Councils in the Region Bremen" where (European) works councils, trade union representatives, experts, colleagues from further education units and other interested parties meet regularly to exchange information and to discuss mutually agreed topics.

In Germany, the project co-operated with the following trade unions: IG Metall (Metalworkers' Union), IG Bergbau-Chemie-Energie (Miners, Chemical and Energy Workers' Union), IG Bauen-Agrar-Umwelt (Construction, Agricultural and Environment Workers' Union), Nahrung-Genuss-Gaststätten (Food and Restaurant Workers' Union) and Handel, Banken und Versicherungen (Commerce, Bank and Insurance Workers' Union).

Co-operation partners in France, Great Britain and Italy were: Adelheid Hege, Christian Dufour and Ingrid Artus from the Institut De Récherches Economiques Et Sociales (IRES), Paris; Lionel Fulton from the Labour Research Department (LRD), London and B. Cattero, University of Frankfurt/M.

The existing project report was written by the Bremen team and therefore falls into their sphere of responsibility. It follows, to a great extent, the procedure of the study.

After the overview of the system of industrial relations in Germany, France, Great Britain and Italy which follows immediately after this, the theoretical-conceptual framework of the investigation will be set out. This is followed by a detailed examination of the "Europeanisation" of industrial relations themselves.

After that, through a re-appraisal of relevant literature, the present development trends and problems of the national systems of industrial relations in particular are examined.

Following on from this, different national experiences and points of view on the development of industrial relations will be highlighted, and how they became especially clear in discussions with the experts and representatives from trade unions and employers' associations.

From the connection between the national and European level of industrial relations we go straight on to the empirical basis of our case studies carried out in the selected parent companies and subsidiaries in the various countries and in the different industrial sectors.

Finally, in thesis-form, we describe the development of industrial relations in Europe as a contradictory process between national and European regulation, which became clear in our study. From this, we shall consider how employees especially and those representing their interests, could be put in a position to take an active rather than a passive role in shaping the process of European Unity.

Thanks go to all those who have helped to ensure the success of this investigation:

- The Hans-Böckler-Foundation and the University of Bremen for their financial sponsorship;
- The corresponding partners in Great Britain, Italy and France for their expertise and the undertaking of the case studies;
- Dr. Michael Braun for carrying out the expert discussions in Rome;
- The representatives of companies and enterprises, trade union and employer associations in the countries involved and at European level, who made themselves available for expert discussions and/or agreed to undertake case studies;
- The European Works Councils, in whose meetings we were allowed to participate as guests;
- The European Trade Union Institute for their guaranteed hospitality;
- Colleagues from companies, trade unions, Institutes of Further Education, and the field of research, who came together with us

- in the "Regional Work Group on European Works Councils" for critical and productive discussions and;
- Henning Schmincke, a student at the University of Bremen, for his assistance during the final stage of the project.

Industrial relations systems in Germany, France, Great Britain and Italy - an overview

With regard to the question of a possible Europeanisation of industrial relations, there has been no shortage of attempts, especially in the last few years, to develop both theoretical constructs of industrial relations in Europe, as well as to draw up related primary and secondary empirical studies (see among others Mesch, 1995; Ferner and Hyman, 1993; Hyman and Ferner, 1995 and Lecher and Platzer, 1994).

The following abbreviated version of the historic development of each national system of industrial relations in our four countries, is also based on these works:

In this scheme, which necessarily refers mainly to institutions and less to industrial relations in each country as a social process, Germany and the UK can be characterised, as extreme poles, between which, with some modifications, Italy and France can be ranked.

Müller-Jentsch (1995) summarises the specific structures and characteristic features of the German system of industrial relations under the following five main points:

- Duality: two different structures of collective bargaining autonomy and co-determination;
- Intermediacy: social institutions and programmes for pragmatic negotiations between capital and labour;
- Legalisation: close network of mainly procedural regulations and legal restrictions on industrial conflicts and industrial action;
- Centralisation: the organisations representing capital and labour have reciprocally encouraged the concentration and centralisation of their associations;
- Representation: organs of collective worker representation, especially those of the employees, have a representative character.

This system ensures that the workplace itself is not normally an area of conflict, but to a large extent carries on production undisturbed.

It is a well-known fact that the most important institutions of this system are the trade unions, the works constitution and with its essential expression, the works council, as well as co-determination at company level.

The trade unions are mainly organised according to the principle of a single industrial union. At the workplace, especially in large concerns, the union structure is based on representatives, who are voted in by trade union members at the workplace.

Overall then, these institutions operate in a fully developed network of industrial labour and social regulations, which together characterise the German system of industrial relations.

The following general tendencies in the historical development of German industrial relations can be observed (Braun, Eberwein and Tholen, 1992, pp. 428 ff.; as well as Eberwein, 1992):

- Liberalisation and objectivation of the power relationship: generally it is true that the relationship of control between capital and labour has not been eliminated. However, the exercise of control was systematised and to a certain extent, rationalised, and in practice the results of this system were liberalised too, i.e. principally were made the object of negotiations and the reconciliation of interests.
- Thematically differentiated and step-by-step process of regulation of potential conflict between capital and labour: industrial relations comprise a network of institutions to overcome and regulate social conflicts. These institutions mean that potential social conflicts are taken apart, divided up and handled on different levels. Thus, conflicts are robbed of the explosive nature that the system might not be able to handle and this allows a different partial solution to be found to these "broken-down complex problems".

The essential difference between the British system of industrial relations and the German one is that in the former, there is no functional and institutional separation of free collective bargaining and regulations governing industrial relations, so there is a single structured system of worker representation. (see amongst others Eberwein and Tholen, 1993, pp. 201-31; Lane, 1995). A counterpart to the German works council generally does not exist. Instead, worker representation in the plant is taken up by shop stewards, i.e. plant trade union representatives who are in effect a combination of German works council member and trade union negotiator. Added to this, as a rule, the shop stewards in a plant or company do not, as in Germany, belong to only one trade union. Rather, shop steward committees are composed of several, sometimes even a multitude of trade unions. This is because British trade unions, as opposed to the German ones, are not in the main structured along industry lines, although considerable changes can be observed. Next to the industrial trade unions there are also professional trade unions and general trade unions. As a consequence of such a workplace-based trade union structure, conflict between management and unions is often focused at the workplace.

Co-determination at the company level like the German system does not exist in Great Britain that is to say it has only made weak beginnings with steering committees in a few large companies, comparable to the German combined works council or general works council, which are generally led by full-time convenors (Lecher, 1997, p. 14).

Finally, Great Britain does also not have the fully-developed network of industrial and social legislation regulations which exists in Germany. However, many things in Britain have resulted from rapid economic and structural change, as well as the political shifts of emphasis since 1979 (the beginning of Thatcherism). Thus, for example the heart of industrial relations, "collective bargaining", declined significantly in importance, the number of trade union members fell rapidly and consequently so did the extent of trade union influence at the workplace. The result is that the idea of co-operation between capital and labour is not being so vehemently rejected by companies, nor by trade unions, to the same extent that it was at the beginning of the 1980s and this therefore favours the occasional formation of works councils along with voluntary agreements of the European Works Council.

In comparison to Great Britain, industrial relations in France have, as in Germany, a different legal basis. Thus, worker representation in the plant is covered by legislation too, but differently from Germany, and is characterised by its three-part structure (Lecher, 1994a, p. 185):

- workforce delegates (délégués du personnel), form a workplace complaints body which has the right to represent the interests of employees collectively and individually, however, it does not have a mandate for collective bargaining. So the workforce delegates have to deal with the day-to-day problems and needs of employees - the closest comparison are the works negotiators in the German chemistry industry (Lecher 1994a, p. 188).
- works committees (comités d'entreprise) are voted in by the work force, and are chaired by a plant representative; they have information and consultation rights to administer workplace social

institutions (social funds). These committees concentrate more on social and cultural activities and so cannot be treated as a functional counterpart of the German works councils.
- trade union delegates (délégués syndicaux), a purely trade union body and the only representative body at plant level that can negotiate a collective agreement.

As a result of the split between representational bodies at plant level, the ability of French trade unions to co-ordinate things at the workplace is more important than in Germany (Lecher, 1994a, pp. 191 f.), although this is limited by the pluralistic divisions in the French trade union movement at national level: in all there are five trade union federations acknowledged as representative and three major direction trade unions.

Collective bargaining takes place regularly between representatives of employer associations and trade unions at different levels, although here, too, there are considerable differences due to historic traditions and legal developments: in France, the ability to take strike action at the workplace is regarded as an indicator of trade union strength, with strikes often held at the beginning of pay disputes; in Germany they are held at the end mostly as a last resort. In addition, in France there is a legally attested right to strike and therefore the socio-political importance of strikes in determining behaviours is a lot greater than in Germany. Furthermore, free collective bargaining plays a considerably larger role in Germany than in France, where the state takes a larger role with a detailed and cleverly thought-out system for influencing pay levels (for instance, by setting the minimum wage and the level of working hours, but especially through informal and political influence). Of course, this begs the question whether a reduction of state control of the French economy would go along with a decrease of state influence in a pay dispute. What has to be taken into account is that trade unions are very weakly represented, especially in the private sector.

In contrast to Germany, where industrial relations are characterised by a fully-developed system which acts to break down conflicts, in France the workplace is generally the focus of a fundamental confrontation between workers and management (Lecher, 1994a, p. 192). Patriarchalism, with its symbol of the "boss", characterises the French employers' approach to controlling the workplace. Workplace representatives are expected to teach workers the boss's view of things, which is, in short that the interests of management are identical with those of the company and these ought to be the interests of the workforce too. When disputes flare up - and this is not exactly rare - many top management representatives are convinced that they have been brought in from outside and mostly by the trade unions. In Germany, however, it is natural that management, too, besides common interests of course, has its own interests that have to be negotiated.

In France, trade union membership sets the workforce apart not only from management, but also from non-organised colleagues.

This is expressed, in the main, by the fact that trade union activities in the workplace mean an end to career promotions - consequently, open trade union support becomes a political question. This, too, is different from the German system.

Cleff, in his empirical study, explains such differences between France and Germany with the stress on intercultural norms and values and their influence on industrial relations. According to him, in contrast to what happens in Germany, the French aspire to an idea of worker participation which manifests itself in the more individualistic and authority-related conduct of the French (Cleff, 1994).

If one follows Hege and Dufour (1995), who regard industrial relations primarily as a social process, there are, however significant parallels between Germany and France with regard to structures and options: the workplace representatives (must) try to overcome the formal dualism of worker representation in their day-to-day practice and their long-term aims.

Concerning the possible Europeanisation of the French industrial relations, reference should be made to the comités du groupes (combined works councils), which have existed in the big state companies in particular since the middle of the 1980s. They are - or are supposed to be - European bodies and committees whose purpose is to gather and exchange information on an international level (Euro-Form or Committee) (Lecher and Platzer, 1996, p. 507). However, in our critical assessment, the comité du groupes only have a very low level of legitimisation: they have weak links with the trade unions and do not co-ordinate the individual companies in a group of companies. It will be important for future developments to see whether the well-developed information and communication methods in French workplaces can be adopted by the EWC (Lecher, 1997, p. 10).

All in all, the French system resembles the German one in terms of legislation, at least formally. In contrast, it is characterised by a basic tendency towards conflict, as is the English one (Lecher and Platzer, 1996, p. 508). "Co-management", as is customary in Germany, is unthinkable for French employers.

In Italy, there was considerable change in industrial relations in the 1980s. This did not proceed quite as spectacularly as 1969 with its "hot autumn", but did produce definite comparative results. Not only at a micro, but also at a macro level organisational relations changed, developing towards a 'silent political exchange/arrangements on a centralised level and towards a decentralised co-operationism at company level' (Ferner and Hyman, 1993, p. 526).

As such, after, amongst other things, the passing/revising of the statuto dei lavoratori of 1993 (rappresentanza sindacali unitarie, RSU), there is only trade union representation at the workplace. The central task of union representatives is the co-ordination and implementation of national wage agreements at plant level. They also have the right to information in certain areas, for instance, market and production prospects, investment plans, employment perspectives and the introduction of new technology.

Collective bargaining occurs between representatives of the respective trade unions and the employer associations at different levels. There are three representative trade union associations in Italy, in which individual trade unions have come together, which in turn are organised by their sector or industry. Alongside these associations, are autonomous trade unions and the so-called basis committees (COBAS), which operate in the public services sector in particular. Due to the changing economic and political situation, the three main trade union associations work together much more closely than they did even say 15 years ago. Recently there has been a considerable increase in the number of collective organisations and in industrial action among highly qualified groups of employees, particularly in the public sector, independent of and often in opposition to the trade unions (Ferner and Hyman, 1993, p. 592) and towards which the trade unions must exercise restraint.

In Italian industrial relations, the paradox is that on the one hand observers see a weakness in the institutions, but on the other that these institutions seem strong enough to determine the direction of change and the limits of possible alternatives (Ferner and Hyman, 1993, p. 593).

It is questionable whether this is applicable to the possible Europeanisation of industrial relations: Lecher and Platzer (1996, p. 510) and Lecher (1997, pp. 19 ff.) assume that in Italy, the chances of a European Works Council operating successfully are greater than in Great Britain or France, on the basis of the development of the first signs of a dualistic system (see especially the RSU) and the narrowing of differences between the politically aligned trade unions. Ferner and Hyman (1993, p. 594) too, have a tendency to see Italian industrial relations as relatively open to Europeanisation influences.

The following table shows a summary of the different systems of industrial relations:

Table 1.1 Industrial relations in Germany, France, Great Britain and Italy

Levels	Germany	GB	France	Italy
Level 1: Form of conflict regulation	Conflict model	Conflict model	Conflict model Micro-corporatism	Co-operation or Consensus model
Level 2: Degree of codification	Bargaining process	Codification	Partial codification	Codification
Level 3: Type of organisation by trade union	Heterogeneity of trade unions	Pluralistic multitude of trade unions	Pluralistic multitude of trade unions	Unity union/ industrial union
Union density in % (approx.)	31	9	44	29
Level 4: Relationship between trade union and workplace representation	Monism Single-structure	Three-level structure -delegués de personnel -comités d'entreprise -delegués syndicaux	Dualism Two-level structure -unified trade union representation in the plant (RSU) -trade union	Dualism Two-level structure -works council -trade unions

This short overview of the developments in research on the institution as, and the regulation of, the industrial relations system in the four named countries makes it clear that an analysis from a comparative standpoint promises to provide considerable insight into the way they function and the processes of change.

A prerequisite for this is a theoretical-conceptual framework, which will be outlined in the following chapter.

2. The process of Europeanisation and the development of industrial relations - theories

The term "Europeanisation"

In order to be able to understand and judge the development of industrial relations in Europe in comparison with the development of national industrial relations, it is necessary to recall the process of European integration. Only by doing so, is it possible to make statements about future perspectives. Starting from the different branches of political theories of integration, with varieties of federalism and neo-functionalism playing an important part, it is predicted that , there will be a further development of the European integration. If this fails, then a marked disintegration and return to nationalism is expected in Europe. Despite minor differences in detail, these positions correspond in that European integration is heading for a final state which has not been reached yet. The political implications are the demand for a "United States of Europe" or the creation of a political union.

Theories of economic integration refer in particular to the transaction cost approach and versions of international trade theory. According to this, the economy, striving of its own accord, towards internationally structured relations, is suppressed by state regulations, leading to a loss in welfare. This theoretical concept aims for the creation of a unified economic area, where, however, the final objective is in principle complete globalisation. Consequently, integration is understood as a basic economic tendency heading for a final state - the global free market.

A consequence of this view is the assumption that, gradually all major areas which up to now have been regulated at a national level or in which the national government has been the leading political protagonist, are (should be) transferred to the European level. Objections to this are seen as obstacles to be overcome - such as the cultural identity of nations or national states and the legitimation of the prevailing political system. In terms of industrial relations, the question arises how will the eventually inevitable European system of industrial relations be conceived and what steps must be taken to realise it. The present situation is seen as a transitional, one which will be overtaken and raised to a new qualitative level by increasing Europeanisation. In this context the question is often asked, which elements of the respective national models of industrial relations will prevail in Europe. These questions actually refer to theories which regard industrial relations as something shaped less by cultural and national characteristics, than by economic and technological constraints.

Our understanding of industrial relations in Europe differs from these politically normative views on the basis of newer research on integration theory.

> The quintessence of today's knowledge concerning the process of European integration is, that it will, most probably never or at least not in the foreseeable future, end in a supranational state structure comparable to post-war state structures, which were able to remove social minima from competition (Streeck, 1998, p. 3).

After the Second World War, there was a move to create a community of European countries because of the system of competition of systems and motivated by peace-politics within the western European countries and more recently since the mid-80s motivated by an increasing internationalisation of the economy and the formation of the triad of North America, South East Asia and Europe. This does not lead to the formation of a new supranational state, but to the co-existence of national, intergovernmental and supranational regulatory structures and authorities. Despite integration,

> we cannot talk of an increasing uniformity of national systems as the outcome of the Europeanisation of politics. All in all, we can see that the process of creating one community allows for a more diversely shaped political landscape within the member states, and especially in those states with a strong tradition of national regulation it leads to a greater complexity (Jachtenfuchs and Kohler-Koch, 1996, p. 28).

In the wake of this development, a new quality of state government emerges, whereby:

> the European level of state government does not merely change according to the national level, but (...) as 'central meeting-point' takes on a major

function as the state government in Europe changes (Ziltener, 1999, p. 202).

This change is closely connected with the new demands on state regulations arising from changed social conditions, which are often described in terms of globalisation, post-fordism and the like. While the state government that was formed in the wake of post-war social and economic developments was limited on a national basis, since the mid-seventies there have been clear instances where national authority has been eroded. The path from "Keynesian welfare state" to the "national competition state" (Hirsch) led in western Europe over the crucial changes and additions of state government through European integration.

The new integration strategy, ratified for the first time in the United Europe Treaty played an important role in these changes. Since the mid-80s the European Union has been shaped mainly by 'negative integration' measures. This means, the forming of the community was achieved less through active measures of European unification and the passing of European laws compulsory for all countries (positive integration), but rather by dismantling barriers and by mutual recognition of national regulation. In the wake of this, integration in various areas of integration was dominated by economic factors and competition emerged between regimes and their national systems.

> As a result, there is a shift in the balance between a capitalistic economic system and a democratically legitimated political system, which emerged in western European welfare states in the post-war years (Scharpf, 1996, p. 110).

This development has to be seen against the background of a significant trend towards neo-liberalism in the member states.

> As a result, following Maastricht, the process of European integration controlled by the national states became the means for European capitalism to escape from state regulation. Even more it became the motivating force for the replacement of a national and state market regime by an international and pre-state regime. National states and the 'markets' didn't allow the regime to become a fully-formed state (Streeck, 1998, p. 5).

So, recently a multi-layered system of state regulation has emerged in Europe - fundamentally different from the system of international relations immediately following the Second World War. When looking at future developments, neither a return to full national state control nor a transformation into a new federal state seems impossible. While economic integration has made great progress and has led to irreversible changes to the structures of member state economies, there are wide areas of state affairs, especially the fields of social and labour politics, which are still organised on a national basis. Because of structural differences and the different levels of economic development among member states, which to a large extent are based on traditions from centuries ago, it seems certain that, in the near future, there will be a close relationship of national and European regulations within a generally close framework.

This situation has not essentially changed even with the advent of European Monetary Union (EMU). As a result of this, economic integration became almost complete, but economic and political support at community level could still not be guaranteed. So far the many attempts to establish more effective co-ordination of economic policy, as demanded by the French government, have failed. The last EU summit produced little of substance despite a great deal of rhetoric. Basically all that was achieved was a stronger co-ordination of labour market policies and a regular - but not obligatory - discussion of the economic policies of member states. In addition, the so-called stability pact was established, which obliges all member states of the EMU to follow a policy of stability, but without ensuring European co-ordination in the narrower sense (tax policies).

There was more a resort to supposedly technocratic mechanisms. This reflected member states' basic consensus on the neo-liberal orientation of their economic policy - which almost all member states' conservative governments developed in the nineties and which was adopted by many of the subsequent social democratic governments. This consensus is not far reaching enough to orchestrate the start of further steps towards harmonisation. It is more a minimal consensus which at the same time reflects the diverse interests.

The supposed lack of regulation within the Maastricht treaty - which concentrates on deepening economic integration and only marginally touches on political integration - results not just from the policies of neo-liberal oriented governments, but also from structural factors, which reflect the prevailing balance of power between members states as well as their diverse interests and those of different social groups.

This has serious consequences for industrial relations, since the exchange rate mechanism as an important mechanism for adjusting the diverse economic developments within the member states has been eliminated by EMU. So the burden of adjustment is transferred from the state's fiscal and structural policy, whose room to manoeuvre is limited by EMU, to collective bargaining policy and industrial relations as well as to social politics. The alternative to this would be diverse developments resulting in real economic adaptations, such as mass unemployment. Industrial relations are now facing an increasing need for change because of this. The danger of wage cuts and social dumping is inevitable. The concrete effects of EMU therefore depend fundamentally on the future orientation of politics and consequently on the political and social balance of power within the member states and on a European level. If the extremely restrictive trends in financial politics are continued, the socio-political regulations, which include financial transfers, will be limited to a great extent. On the other hand, an economic policy focussing on promotion of employment and more effective co-ordination would reduce the pressure on pay and social policy.

When looking at integration from this perspective, it becomes clear that the term "Europeanisation" does not stand for a steadily progressing unification at a European level nor does it stand for a simple transposition of national settlements onto settlements of the European Union. Europeanisation stands more for the establishment of a new interconnecting structure, concerned with political, economic and social regulations, which out of necessity must be presented differently in each country. Consequently the term 'Europeanisation' implies three dimensions:

- the establishment of European regulation with means of positive and negative integration;
- changes in regulation in the countries affected; and
- a change of interdependency between national, supra-national and sub-national levels of regulation.

Consequences for socio-political regulation

It is not possible to draw the conclusion from the facts mentioned above, that socio-political integration, which includes the regulation of industrial relations, will remain at the current level. Partial progress is possible from the point of view of an expansion of European regulation.

Since the mid-80s an exceptional feature of socio-political integration has emerged from the new integration strategy, which Platzer refers to as 'negotiated Europeanisation'. By this he means the partial retreat of state-run or governmental institutions from their regulatory role in social politics and industrial, which in many countries is normal within the framework of free collective bargaining. Within the framework of the "social dialogue", for example, employers and unions have the opportunity to negotiate over regulations which will be legally valid throughout Europe. It is controversial to what extent this negotiated Europeanisation will be of material significance. In some people's view, it is essential for the further development of the social dimension. Others are more sceptical in the light of the hitherto limited results of the social dialogue and its perspectives.

A further deepening of the socio-political aspects of integration may be expected In spite of the inadequate results, in socio-political terms, from the revision of EU contracts in the 1990s. Platzer argues correctly that progress towards extensive economic integration has always led to an examination of the need for european regulation in other political areas. The level of socio-political regulation has always lagged behind economic regulation.

> Nevertheless the development of the "social dimension", even if shifted back a stage, partially shifted in its phases, does lead to greater regulation in terms of guidelines and decrees as well as and transfer-political checking lists. But it is also expressed in an increase in 'soft' means of co-ordination such as reports, declarations, recommendations, guidelines etc. (Platzer, 1999, p. 181).

All in all, the development of industrial relations in Europe will not lead to European standardisation. Strategies which declare this as their aim, explicitly or implicitly, can only fail. What we can expect is that, while the dominance of national regulation is maintained, some differentiation will arise, whereby the different systems of industrial relations will be supplemented with European regulation and there will also be changes within the national systems themselves. Politically, strategically, the trade unions will have to find solutions to the question of how to formulate the principle of subsidiarity in terms of industrial relations. So it is about deciding which regulations are to be negotiated exclusively on the European level, how national systems must be developed, how the relationship between the different levels should be formulated and which European regulations should be restricted in order to make further national regulation possible.

In order to be able to determine this transition more closely, we need to refer to theories of industrial relations.

Industrial relations theory

At this point, it is not necessary to look at the whole field of industrial relations theory. Following Mueller-Jentsch, there is a framework of analysis for the project at hand, which refers to several theoretical themes:

As a theoretical guideline for presenting and analysing the relevant facts for industrial relations, I propose an extended, subject-orientated, institutionalised approach; an integration of historic and control-orientated institutionalism with action-theoretical (mainly negotiating) concepts. The approach consists of three theoretical "basic elements":

1. The historic-genetic analysis,
2. The concept of arenas, and
3. The concept of negotiation (Mueller-Jentsch, 1996, p. 57).

This approach has the advantage of recording different moments of determination in the dynamic. In this context, the concrete form of linking and evaluating the different elements remains an unsolved theoretical problem. At the same time, this differentiation appears to be sufficient to record the diverse qualities and functions of industrial relations at the different levels of multi-level regulation within the framework of the EU.

The historical, genetic analysis refers to the evolutionary character of industrial relations, where the specific conditions in each country have led to different national systems emerging. Therefore, each country has its own path of development, which manifests itself in particular in institutional structures and the patterns of behaviour of those involved.

Nonetheless, a typical pattern of development and generalised results applicable to all industrial capitalistic countries in the west can be noted (Mueller-Jentsch, 1996, p. 57).

In the end, similarities emerge from the functional requirements arising from the system of industrial relations which is based on the economic necessities of capitalistic economies.

The concept of arenas refers to the functional differentiation of industrial relations and therefore to the division of different sub-systems. In spite of all their links, those sub-systems have a relative autonomy in the field of dispute. Finally, the concept of negotiation includes in its analysis the actions of the participants and the way they develop their strategies.

The pressure for change in the face of globalisation and the assertion of new forms of production and work

In Europe over the last 200 years quite different systems of industrial relations have emerged in each country. These now face a need for extensive change. Two developments are mainly responsible for this: the increasing globalisation[1] of the economy and the emergence of new means of production and new ways of working.

A basic aspect of industrial relations in European countries has been its national limits. Despite being export-orientated and despite the level of international transactions, businesses still treat national economic structures as their basic point of reference. Economic and social politics could only function if, to some extent, they were sealed off from the world market. This was the context in which pay bargaining systems and the business world have developed. With growing globalisation, the foundations of this system are being eroded.

Internationalisation of the economy is being carried out above all by transnational firms (with medium-sized enterprises increasingly being involved) with several production centres in different countries. These companies try to organise production and sales in an optimal way, making use of diverse national conditions. An essential condition of the increased room for manoeuvre for these companies is the conscious political decision to deregulate the world economy. Taking advantage of these opportunities has another consequence. The fact that companies' can choose the best production centres, increases the significance of local factors. So, parallel to the globalisation process, the regions as sub-national units are of growing importance, as factors for production but also as levels of political control.

This growing internationalisation has far-reaching consequences. Deregulation - as promoted widely by neo-conservative governments - has produced a range of new competitive pressures along with social divisions which together have helped fundamentally to weaken trade unions as well as undermining the scope for intervention at national level. Conservative, supply-side economic policies mean that national states now compete with each other to cut costs in order to give their local economies a competitive advantage. According to this way of thinking, the welfare state as well as a range of other political and economic are simply costs that should be cut back in order to support the local economy. This is the start of a downward spiral. This combination of factors leads to the emergence of new social divisions.

Industrial relations systems are already under immense pressure as a result of the trend to globalisation and this will increase with the impact of new production technologies and associated patterns of rationalisation. Businesses are undergoing fundamental reorganisation as a result of new

---

[1] The term globalisation is imprecise and is a matter of debate from both a technical and political point of view. In the context of this report, it is not necessary to define the term precisely. It refers to the considerable expansion of international economic transactions in connection with changes in company structures in an international context.

information and communications technologies. Reorganisation is not just affecting specific levels in the chain of production but the links in the chain as a whole. There is a move away from Taylor's paradigm of rationalisation, which is particularly aimed at increasing the efficiency of particular stages in the production process by breaking production through increasing use of technology. The guideline for the new paradigms which are taking over is 'systematic rationalisation' which aims at optimising the whole of the production process, in particular the interfaces between different steps of production. According to Dörre (1995, pp. 155f.) three levels of reorganisation can be distinguished in the abstract:

- strengthening market orientation at the expense of mechanisms of management co-ordination;
- reorganisation of management structures in terms of levelling out management hierarchies, including the cutting out of individual layers of management; and
- introducing teamwork on the 'shop floor' in order to integrate work and functions.

How these restructuring measures are realised in practice differs widely depending on the industrial sector and the individual firm. Popular buzzwords in this context include "lean production", "just-in-time production" and "out-sourcing". It should be noted that such measures are often carried out in sectors facing increased competition or sectors in decline. Therefore, the significance of cost cutting for businesses should not be underestimated, and this is of great importance for possible design options. In this respect, one often talks about the replacing fordist structures of production, especially mass production and the transition towards a post-fordistic, flexible and quality-orientated system of production. To some extent this characterisation neglects the fact that emerging forms of production are still mass production and that flexible industrial production is concerned with single components. For example, in the car industry it is possible to choose between cars with different components, so, in fact few cars are really identical. However, in fact the variation between individual components is limited.

These measures have a considerable impact on trade union and workplace representatives.

> Processes of reorganisation encourage a tendency towards workplace-based representation and regulation in the plant. This happens because the implementation of different forms of rationalisation requires solutions that are based on concrete processes of work. It is also becoming increasingly

apparent that all attempts to create flexibility in work organisation necessarily have an impact on the control of working conditions, salary, working hours and so on (Dörre, 1995, pp. 158f.).

In particular the system of workers' participation set out in the German Works Constitution Act is inadequate for the changes in management connected to new patterns of rationalisation to be implemented. The present regulations:

> are limited to a large degree by certain conditions (covering working hours and performance monitoring) or special restrictions resulting from technical and organisational measures. (...) So, from the legal point of view, the position of trade unions in terms of their control over work organisation can be characterised as defensive, reactive and aiming at defending workers and trade unions from the social impact of reorganisation. Current legal conditions mean that the expansion of co-determination to cover technology and management is only possible on the basis of 'voluntary' arrangements with the employer (Helfert, 1992, p. 505).

These general tendencies will be dealt with in the following text together with the specific conditions and structures in various European countries.

Europeanisation of industrial relations as a restructuring of the regulatory hierarchies and a change in national systems

A variety of systems of industrial relations have developed over time in different countries.

A concept of the Europeanisation of industrial relations can be developed against the background of the complexity of industrial relations in each country and the process of integration as characterised above. This cannot be simply reduced to a question of the degree of collective or legal regulation at the European level nor to the question of an increasing convergence of the systems. Europeanisation can only be understood as a complex process of:

- a new order of levels of regulation;
- a change of function as well as a change of subsystems; and
- a reaction to the challenges of economic globalisation and the implementation of new methods of production.

Of special interest in terms of a theoretical understanding of the Europeanisation of industrial relations is the question of what functions will be carried out at the European level and what institutions will emerge as a consequence. In terms of Platzer's "negotiated Europeanisation", one must bear in mind in particular that a European level of regulation works specifically in connection with the given national systems of industrial relations. The effectiveness of European regulation can only be assessed if the national interconnections are taken into consideration.

3. Selected empirical findings on the development of industrial relations in Europe[2] - current research

As a result of the signing of the Maastricht treaty, an increasing number of empirical studies of the development of industrial relations in Europe were carried out. The central aim of these studies was to assess the effects of European integration and economic internationalisation on industrial relations. Moreover several recent studies deal with the most distinctive institution of European industrial relations - European works councils. In the following chapter, we want to outline a few fundamental theses from these studies.

Plant and company levels

The Europeanisation of plant and company level industrial relations as a consequence of European integration?

In order to determine the political and strategic importance of European Works Councils (EWCs), it is necessary to analyse the underlying trends, which influenced union demands to set them up. The progress of Europeanisation and the implicit Europeanisation of enterprises are outlined as part of the argument, followed by the creation of further possibilities for company-level co-determination. In our interpretation EWCs are a part of the social dimension of the EU, which needs to go through a considerable catching-up process. As mentioned above, these arguments about the theory of integration are not conclusive. In addition,

---

[2] Although the focus is on studies in Germany they are not limited to Germany and include other countries.

empirical researchers point out that despite a major wave of concentration and centralisation within the EU, there is fairly slow progress in the formation of European companies that is in the sense of a decreasing dominance of national parent companies and establishment of multinational, European parent companies. After all, most companies are still British, French, Italian, and German.

To a certain extent it is not enough to refer to a missing social dimension in order to justify the setting up of EWCs. In the literature, two closely linked tendencies will be analysed which lead to fundamental changes in industrial relations in individual countries.These are the increasing internationalisation of the economy combined with the introduction of new forms of labour organisation, both of these being based on new technology, especially information and communication technology.

Employee representation in international companies

The studies by Koubeck and others called 'Company Strategies in the Triad' examine the correlation between changing company strategies in the chemical industry, as a result of internationalisation and attempts to optimise the production lines/processes, and the possibilities for action by worker representatives. According to Koubeck and others, following improvements in the production process, companies aim to concentrate their activities in core areas, which leads to an emphasis on developing strategies focusing on a company's specific areas of business. Consequently three diverse and fundamental strategic decisions are combined. In terms of internationalisation this means choosing between the following options:

"Concentration on one world region", "Internationalisation with the main emphasis on regional aspects of the world" and "Internationalisation with a global orientation". At the same time, there is the potential to optimise production lines at the final product stage, the pre-product stage or throughout the whole production process. The company's choice of location and impact on internal competition between groups of employees will vary according to which combination of strategies is chosen. The authors conclude that the combination of specific strategies based on internationalisation and improvements in a line of production do not necessarily result in a regional relocation of whole production processes.

> This implies the conclusion, that - contrary to many views on the subject - developing countries are not necessarily a more attractive location for basic chemicals production than industrialised countries, if full advantage is taken of the proximity to the market of purchasing industries in creating competitive cost structures (Koubeck and others, 1996, p. 24).

But in order to achieve this, companies need a specific sector-orientated set of strategies. Against this background, the authors recommend that worker representation has a sector-based structure, which is set up to support the company's competitive potential. Worker representation strategies based on co-management of this kind have been developed against a background of changes in competitive conditions. Taking into account the diverse material requirements of production processes of course, they can be applied to many sectors that are integrated in competitive world markets within the three-bloc framework. These strategies of worker representation require a reliable source of information at an international level and an international or at least European-level structure of information and worker representation.

In his research, covering a period up to 1991, Mertens puts a different emphasis on the international co-operation of worker representatives in VW. In his work, he assumes:

> that the establishment of co-operative contacts between workers' organisations depends on the increasing competition between groups of employees which leads to a decline in the effectiveness of the worker organisations affected. But this co-operation has to limit the factors that have a negative impact on the effectiveness of worker organisations (Mertens, 1994, p. 3).

According to Mertens the increase in competition is, on the one hand, related to the internationalisation of the company's structure, which is followed by an increase in competition inside the company. On the other hand it is also due to a general increase in competition, caused, for example, by the removal of national borders in the EU and the formation of a single market. So in terms of VW, he notes an increased level of international competition, which impacts upon other car manufacturers. But statements about internal competition in the company can only be made on the basis of an analysis of the company's strategy. From Mertens' point of view, the EWC is an institutionalised forum of co-operation intended for workers organisations. Mertens believes that the institutionalisation of co-operation is of great importance, since it is a stabilising factor and therefore the basis for permanent co-operation. Noting the EWC's limited influence, Mertens says that it can only deal with some of the causes of increasing competition. The inadequate results of the social dialogue or social politics within the EU have a negative impact on competition. Co-operation of companies at a company level has limited scope for confronting these problems.

The impact of changes in labour organisation

There are four other studies comparing international changes in labour organisation and their impact on worker representation (Krieger and Fröhlich, 1998; Lawerino, 1996/97; Müller-Jentsch, Sperling and Weyrather, 1997 and Volz, 1997). In all four studies, the authors come to the conclusion that at an international level there are clear similarities in the basic direction of the strategies adopted by organisations. To a certain extent a convergence of industrial relations can be found in numerous areas.

> When summarising the diversity of negotiation processes and their outcomes, it becomes apparent, that despite the continued existence of diverse systems of negotiation - which are at the same time going through changes - there is a tendency for bargaining strategies and emerging patterns of participation to converge (Müller-Jentsch, Sperling and Weyrather, 1997, p. 231).

You can find this tendency towards greater flexibility and participation in all kinds of industries. As a result traditional industrial relations are put under pressure. The relationship between direct and indirect workplace representation has to be adjusted. In this context, increasing international competition plays a significant role. But it is apparent from all the studies that the processes of adaptation differ from country to country and that they are substantially influenced by the prevailing system of industrial relations and conflicts between trade unions, management and employers or employers' associations.

> It is apparent that on the one hand multinational companies put forward a range of measures to increase (...) flexibility and offers of participation. On the whole these companies display a similar orientation at a "strategic" level, but show considerable diversity at a local level (Volz, 1997, p. 100).

Müller-Jentsch and others eventually draw the conclusion that:

> Industrial relations are embedded in national and cultural traditions and in historically developed institutions. Future development depends on what happened in the past. Historical breaks from the past and radical changes of systems are an exception. Therefore we can predict with some certainty, that the development will not lead to a convergence towards a uniform European model of industrial relations (Müller-Jentsch, Sperling and Weyrather, 1997, p. 236).

The EWC as a contradictory response to Europeanisation

Against the background of this research the role of the EWC seems ambivalent. On the one hand, it is a basic European institution of industrial relations, especially since collective bargaining at a European level is not in reach and since the social dialogue remains ineffective because of the negative approach from the employers. Next to the work of European employers and trade union federations, the EWC is the key committee aiming for co-operation at a European level. As Mertens correctly remarks, the EWC only covers one part of industrial relations, namely worker representation at the workplace.

On the other hand, the studies point out that the inadequate legislation is not the only reason why the EWC despite the name work council does not have much in common with works councils in the sense of the German Works Constitution Act. It has a very small role in European industrial relations. Industrial relations still operate at a national level, even though there is a tendency towards change as a result of new forms of labour organisation and a process of internationalisation leading to similar changes in different countries. The EWC will not play an independent role - at least not in the near future. It will only make an impact in as far as it relates to each country's system of industrial relations. This view is also supported by Lecher/Platzer. They both believe that the EWC is a core element in developing European industrial relations and so they emphasise the urgency of establishing a much closer connection with national systems of industrial relations (Lecher and Platzer, 1996; Lecher, 1998).

After all, European Works Councils reflect the contradictory nature of the Europeanisation of industrial relations and the dialectical interrelationship between national and international systems.

Another important point in this exposition is the fact that trade unions have not yet arrived at a generally accepted political or strategic view of EWCs. So far they have focused their attention on establishing committees, without really knowing what these committees should be used for. The majority of employers generally reject EWCs, considering them to be superfluous. This is why EWCs are more a potential rather than an actual factor in industrial relations.

Deficiencies of the EWC

Legislation on EWCs is not at all uniform. There are considerable differences in the way the EU-directive has been transposed into national law; this is less question of the form than of the material content of the directive. In principle, no standard European legislation was developed, and so sixteen variations emerged, with only a uniform orientation and framework provided for by the EU-directive (Buschak, 1998).

There is a wide range of EWC agreements because no clear direction is given by the guidelines and national laws leaving management and unions a completely free hand to manoeuvre.

It would be wrong to condemn these differences in legislation as a deficiency in EWCs since the diverse national systems of industrial relations can only be connected to such a European institution in a very specific way. From the German point of view, it must be emphasised that due to the legislation, the EWC does not represent a fourth, specifically European level of co-determination, but is more an independent body, which in some ways is comparable to the economic committee (Wirtschaftsausschuss) in the German workplace constitution. Starting from this point, it is possible to determine what legal deficiencies there are - although only from the point of view of industrial relations in Germany. In the literature, EWCs are often criticised for not being based on co-determination. If this is their supposed purpose, then of course the directive is completely inadequate. If one agrees that due to diverse cultures of co-determination in the other European countries, the EWC could not be a body based on co-determination, then other criteria for evaluation must be used. In this case, there are inherent deficits in the inadequate legal requirements in terms of "information" and "consultation" as well as ambiguous and inadequate regulations concerning the involvement of trade unions or external experts.

The various empirical reports on the work of EWCs work provide some help in creating a clearer picture. First of all it has to be said that most EWCs have only existed for about three years with just a few meetings taking place each year, so the lack of experience is apparent. That is why most of the empirical reports refer to the period when the EWCs were set up rather than to the work of the EWCs themselves. While there is a variety of agreements establishing European works councils, there is evidence of a prevailing company culture as well as a willingness by management to agree an practical policy on information and consultation. However, reports on the experiences of EWCs indicate that in practice things are very different. The individual commitment and competence of each participant has considerable bearing on the process and effectiveness of the work of the EWC (Höland, 1997). You can find examples of extensive co-operation - even on the level of the EWC - at VW and at the Digital Equipment Corporation (DEC). Here, the attempt was made to use the EWC via worker representation as the negotiation body, where even locational questions were discussed. For VW, we do not have any information on the material success of this policy. At DEC, the strategy eventually failed due to the sale of the company. It still had positive effects on solidarity across different locations (Mertens, 1994; Müller, 1998). At Danone (formerly BSN) four framework agreements on so-called soft topics (additional training due to new technology, establishing an adequate information policy, equal opportunities for men and women, guarantee of trade union rights) were passed, which serve as guidelines for management at each location. It is not known to what extent these central guidelines were put into practice (Danone, 1997).

A fundamental problem of co-operation is the lack of language skills among trade unions and the lack of information about industrial relations in other countries.

Another weakness of the work of EWCs is - due to their recent foundation - the considerable uncertainty among trade unions about which strategic aims should be pursued. Very often management believes that the EWC does not make any sense at all. And finally, there is also a large number of companies where an EWC could be set up but where, very often as a result of trade union passivity, nothing has been done, demonstrating that the lack of a strategic view is also a major shortcoming. In addition, management often attempts to avoid setting-up EWCs and if this is not possible, they attempt to make the work of EWCs more difficult. Here the imprecise definition of the directive's essential terms - such as "information" and "consultation"- as well as the indistinct definitions referring to the participation of trade unions and external experts - can be seen as a deficit.

Solving problems through the EWC

In a few cases, it is evident that the EWC was able to achieve minor successes. In VW a solidarity network was set up covering different plants, with job security as its main focus. It is not very surprising to find defensive strategies such as job security at the top of the agenda. But despite these positive examples, the emphasis is still on the fact that the EWC basically cannot resolve the tensions between the interests of the local workforce, the interests of employees in other companies and the interests of the group as a whole (Deppe/Hoffmann/Stützel, 1997).

Because of the relatively short time they have been operating, it is not possible to make any general predictions about whether EWCs really have been instrumental in solving problems. But numerous reports refer to one immediate effect of the EWC, especially in foreign subsidiary companies as a result of worker representatives getting information directly from the headquarters for the first time and having a broader source of information than before.

The question is what changes should be made to the directive, to enable the EWC to take on more creative tasks. Again, the empirical reports do not provide answers to these questions. A vision of the EWCs political and strategic purpose is needed to provide a response. In the light of the reality of industrial relations in Europe and their predicted development, it seems very unlikely that EWCs will evolve into bodies based on co-determination. On this basis EWCs should, on the one hand, be established as wide-ranging committees of information. On the other hand, the EWC must serve as a forum for all participating representative groups, especially in order to discuss aspects of company development relevant to specific workplaces. In an ideal case such discussions could lead to the formation of a common position in opposition to the management, which then must be further pursued through the existing national structures.

In formulating such an objective, it would be crucial to extend and express the EWC's legal rights more distinctly. Furthermore the capacity of EWCs for handling and dealing with information should be enlarged. This is of particular concern for the integration of trade union representatives from outside the company and other experts as well for the provision of resources to EWCs. Research by Nagel and others reveals that improvements to EWCs' legal rights alone will not be enough. In many companies the management policy on information is taken as read and forms the basis for the works council's operation. In such a situation, the EWC threatens to become nothing more than an extension of management. In order to avoid this, works councils need to have a more critical approach to the information received and must be willing to produce an independent assessment of the companies' development, although not necessarily one in conflict with the management view (Nagel/Riess/ Rüb/Beschorner, 1996).

The attitude of the employers' associations and trade unions

For many years employers' associations and the governments of some member states opposed the setting up of EWCs. Originally put forward in the 1970s it was not until 1994 that the EWC directive was published. The first European works councils were established in the 1980s but these were exceptional cases. More EWCs were set up on a voluntary basis after the EWC directive was passed but before it came into effect, because many companies decided to commence negotiations and aim for voluntary agreements to avoid being forced to set up an EWC. The major motivation for management to reach a voluntary agreement was to get round the directive's minimum legal requirements. On the whole, management tended to adopt a negative view of EWCs (Stützel, 1996; Blank, Geissler and Jaeger, 1996 or Gerstenberger, 1996).

However, many worker representatives also had reservations about setting up EWCs. This is demonstrated by the fact that many German works councils did not consider initiating the setting up of an EWC. In surveys carried out by the Hans-Boeckler-Stiftung in Germany, 30% of all works councils pointed out that despite having discussed the topic, they did not have any plans to establish an EWC (Deppe, Hoffmann and Stützel, 1996; Stützel, 1996).

Another major problem that has to be overcome in establishing an EWC is the difficulty workers have in dealing with varying custom and practice in industrial relations, as well as general problems of intercultural communication. This often starts with a lack of language skills leading to major difficulties in communication. At the same time workplace representatives usually have a clearly defined view of industrial relations, which often fails to match the daily experiences in other countries. So it usually takes a lot of time to get to know each other, before employees are in a position to work together.

This research does not assess how management deals with these problems. But management studies, focusing on different themes, show that, with the exception of language difficulties, management faces similar problems to those of the employees. The extent of the problems depends on the degree to which a company has an international perspective. Where a company adopts an international perspective and promotes a uniform and international culture throughout the enterprise it will find it more difficult to adjust than where the company's strategy allows individual workplaces to maintain their own culture and where central management expects sites to adhere to predetermined economic guidelines.

Despite these problems, reports of the work of EWCs show that the institution clearly has improved trans-national co-operation between trade unions, because unions are effectively "forced" to co-operate through it. In particular, the European trade union federations, whose role has been considerably strengthened through co-ordinating the various participating unions, have profited from this considerably. The federations very often proved to be the lead organisation both during the negotiations as well as in the actual work of the EWC in practice. This helped to strengthen the federations' position not only internally, but also externally in their relattalions with companies and the EU Commission. At the same time it has increased the number of trade unionists who come into contact with the European federations. The federations are not merely considered on a diplomatic level, but are seen as an essential part of trade union representation in companies.

The development of the trade unions and employers' associations

In summary, the conclusions from a range of studies suggest the following picture of how European trade unions and European employers' associations have developed:

Employers' associations are opposed to the formation of European institutions or European regulation of industrial relations. Here, two aspects seem to be important. First of all, employers' associations think that the outcome of pay and other workplace disputes will be better for them if the pressures of international competition are allowed a free reign. Secondly it is the case that they simply do not have adequate structures on a European level to deal with negotiated agreements.

For the unions, the main point is that EWCs give them a new role to play and so compensates them for the decline in their ability to act at a national level in response to the internationalisation and Europeanisation of enterprises. This is evident in almost all of the studies. The push for a Europeanisation of industrial relations remains focused on national systems. From the German perspective, the setting-up of an EWC is often implicitly seen as a fourth level of co-determination (next to workplace, company, and group levels of co-determination). Foreign trade unions do not share this point of view and neither is it possible to push it through within the present legal framework. So far, a clear political and strategic objective for the EWC has not been formulated.

None of the national unions seem to be willing to had over some of their power to the European federations. This is clear from the limited material support provided to the federations. The federations have been given a co-ordinating role but also to some extent the job of opposing developments that limit the ability to act at a national level. The setting up of EWCs has considerably strengthened the European Trade Union Federations. They were given a role in negotiating EWCs and in the actual running of some EWCs.

Generally one can say that communication between people of different cultures creates fundamental problems which can hamper the process of co-operation. First of all, there are the inadequate language skills which for the time being, can only be dealt with through long-winded translations. According to Lecher and others (1998), a solution is only possible if the parties can agree on a common language.

The second serious problem is a lack of knowledge of the systems of industrial relations in other countries. This is not only a question of the institutional structure, but above all concerns the development of an understanding of the custom and practice in each of the other countries.

Both these factors make it more difficult for trade unions to establish the necessary trust between them and it is only by going through a learning process that they can achieve this. This also means that international co-operation should not be limited to just a few "diplomats" but should involve trade unionist activists at the workplace level. A further problem is the limited number of international meetings bringing together union activists. In some cases it is clear that new media such as the internet can help improve the process of communication.

The existence of a range of different trade unions in each country is another obstacle as it is often unclear who the contact person in the other country is. Political differences between trade unions can also partially undermine the trust necessary for a more effective communication and co-operation.

The significance of collective bargaining at a European level

The empirical studies provide little information on the importance of collective bargaining at a European level. This is mainly because a European wage policy in the narrow sense does not exist. The social dialogue now provides a legal basis for a form of collective bargaining and employer and union organisations can now negotiate agreements in some areas that automatically become valid throughout the EU. In practice the social dialogue has been a disappointment with very few agreements settled so far and the ones that have are of minor importance. This is the result of opposition from employers alongside the failure of different unions to come to agreements and the weaknesses of the trade union federations. In the meantime, there have been hardly any new attempts to draw up European wage agreements, as the emphasis is more on co-ordinating national policies on pay bargaining.

In his evaluation of collective bargaining agreements and changes in collective bargaining in the metal industry in seven countries, Burgess concludes that while there has been some move towards harmonising pay structures, pay determination and collective bargaining are still dominated by national arrangements. He notes a trend towards decentralisation and differentiation, which is evident in different degrees in the countries being studied. These developments are partially due to changes in international competition. Burgess did not report on any (successful) efforts to establish agreements at a European level.

The conclusions made in the project "European wage policy in the construction industry" point in the same direction. In many relevant fields of the construction industry, the wage situation has changed because of the internationalisation and Europeanisation of companies. The high pressure of competition in this sector is less the result of the mobility of production factor capital, but rather a consequence of the increasing mobility of the workforce. Starting out from this development, the construction industry unions increasingly attempted to co-ordinate the wage policy and, if it appeared to make sense, to draw up European settlements. This referred to the passing of a European directive on the dispatching of workers, in which the conditions for posting workers to other EU countries were to be regulated. After efforts to establish a European directive failed, the building trade unions, co-ordinated by the EFBWW tried to establish national settlements.

In the conclusions of this project, Baumann, Laux and Schnepf emphasise the heterogeneity of industrial relations and trade unions in the countries examined. In their opinion the Europeanisation of pay bargaining is desirable, especially in the light of the changes that will arise from monetary union, but they explicitly point out that for the time being, the co-ordinated agreement of standard pay deals in each country will improve the possibilities for unions to restructure. They argue that if unions want to improve their ability to agree pay settlements then they will have to: improve the exchange of information on wage rates and bargaining policies; coordinate bargaining strategies with the strategic political tasks of EWCs; make use of inter-regional trade union bodies as forums of co-ordination; and, where possible, use EU-level regulations to establish basic rights such as the right to strike.

In this case the authors want to establish a legal basis for possible strike action across national borders. At the moment, for example, German workers are not allowed to take the kind of solidarity action shown in the Renault-Vilvoorde case and this is a serious obstacle to achieving solidarity in individual companies throughout Europe.

4. Views from trade unions and employers' associations experts - National and European experiences[3]

Developments at plant and company level

Potential differences between national and Europeanised industrial relations

Industrial relations at plant and company level have been subject to considerable changes in all the countries examined. The increasing internationalisation of companies is undermining systems of worker representation and co-determination which, regardless of their individual characteristics, are important elements of the post-war compromise between Capital and Labour. All these systems are based on a national framework and allow limited scope for international regulation of industrial relations at plant and company level. In the current period of economic and social development, however, the international dimension takes on a considerably higher importance than in the past.

Industrial relations at plant and company level vary considerably in the countries examined. The German model of industrial relations by co-determination at workplace level is based on the Works Constitution Act as well as by co-determination at board level within joint-stock companies (whether they are public limited companies, mining companies or limited liability companies). Here, the main factor is the dual structure of worker

---

[3] These results refer mainly to interviews with representatives of German trade unions and employers' associations or with representatives of their European federations. Additional views, opinions etc. from France, Great Britain and Italy were also included. When assessing the results we have to take into account that the interviewees are experts on European matters.

representation at plant level and trade union at a broader level. In Great Britain, for example, a single structure of worker representation prevails, which does not allow for any co-determination rights in the narrower sense of the word. Access to information and the extent of consultation depend upon the strength of trade unions within each company. In Italy, despite the political divisions among trade unions, a uniform system of worker representation at plant level, dominated by the unions, has been established. This does not provide for any co-determination rights in the narrower sense of the word.

All these systems have immense difficulties coping with individual companies in terms both of the growth in their international operations as well as with an increasing internalisation of their structure and culture. These problems, however, are apparent in very different ways. In Great Britain, for example, the union focus is plant level - and hardly at all at company level. In this context, internationalisation generates the need for new legal regulations to cover worker representation (such as, for example, the transfer into national British law of the European Works Council directive). In Germany, however, internationalisation undermines the decision-making and co-determination structures which are essential for the German system. This, in turn, means the system has to adapt or it becomes ineffective.

> If the basic structures of industrial relations which have developed in each country get into difficulties, as is apparently the case at the moment, then there are only two ways to go: either one tries to isolate the national system in a quasi protectionist manner in order to protect it, or one takes a risk with a leap into the unknown involving transnational co-operation over the basic structure and content of industrial relations systems covering worker representation at company and collective bargaining levels (Lecher, 1998, p. 680).

In the specialised literature, these two courses of action are often contrasted. Streeck, for example, develops an argument based on the assumption that a comprehensive adjustment of the social and industrial relations framework will not take place in the EU. In his view, there will be neither a European "social model" nor a European social union in the foreseeable future. Consequently, he considers it illusory to base political ideas on the assumption that a Europeanisation of social regulations is taking place. On the contrary, the promotion of European integration, given added impetus by neo-liberal tendencies in the 1990s, will lead, 'if it is not successfully counteracted, to a replacement of the European Social State by a configuration which can be defined as a Competition State' (Streeck, 1998, p. 3). In this context, social regulation is subordinate to safeguarding and increasing national competitiveness. In his opinion, counteraction involves allowing for as much regulatory control at national level as possible.

The establishment of "European Works Councils" is according to him an essential cornerstone in creating the competition state.

> These so-called European Works Councils change nothing. Contrary to widely held views, EWCs are basically not about the Europeanisation of the German or any other workplace structures. Instead, they represent one of the most obvious examples of European integration finally moving away from the ideal of a politically harmonised European social state, which is protected against internal competition (Streeck, 1998, p. 8).

He backs up his views with a variety of concrete examples of the limited power of structures at national and plant level. According to Streeck, future changes in the way companies are organised through the planned directive on the structure of a European Company (SE) will have the same effect.

The opposite pole of the debate is formed by authors such as Lecher, Platzer, Keller and Jacobi who explicitly plead for the step-by-step development of a European harmonised social model. Often, with reference to the EMU, they see a considerable factual pressure on Europeanising the social systems which will relativisze the still existing hindrances in a comparably short time. Only if the economic integration were supplemented by a further deepening of the political and social integration would a sufficient legitimisation of the EU be permanently ensured. At the same time, in the step-by-step Europeanisation, a chance would be seen to oppose the reduction of trade union powers caused by internationalisation with a political concept which already in the short and medium-term, would again increase the possibilities for negotiation and structural planning.

On the whole, they admit that so far, it has only been possible to take the first rudimentary steps towards Europeanisation. They feel, however, that the few institutions which have been set up, could trigger a corresponding dynamic in connection with the objective pressure to Europeanize, which would also help to overcome resistance from the part of employers.

> In the relation triangle of the first approaches towards European industrial relations "social dialogue - sectorial dialogue - plant-level dialogue" the European Works Councils form the most dynamic pole (Platzer and Weiner, 1998, p. 410).

This debate forms the background for the following evaluation of our expert interviews which focussed on the following questions:

- What strategic importance is attached to the EWCs?
- What are the experiences of the EWCs in the course of their work and how are these experiences evaluated?
- What repercussions on the national industrial relations are evident?
- How is the planned Europeanisation of company constitution evaluated?

Views of trade unionists and employers' representatives

Points of contact with Europe The policies and attitudes of people active at plant level and in employer associations are influenced by the processes of internationalisation and Europeanisation in general, as well as by their experiences in their own area of work. The way they assimilate these experiences has a considerable impact on their attitudes to and policies on concrete issues.

Alongside sector specific approaches, there are variations as a result of different interests, areas of work and according to the different individual attitudes towards European integration. Sector specific approaches are straightforward and affect employers and trade unionists alike. Thus, mobility of the workforce is a central issue in the construction industry, whereas, for example, regulatory matters play a role in the food industry. Health and safety regulations are of important in all branches of industry and these often originate from or at least are influenced by the EU.

According to trade unionists in the chemical and food industry much of the impetus for Europeanisation comes from the strategies of major companies. These firms increasingly define themselves as European or even global enterprises and thus raise international and European questions with workplace representatives - such as, the development of uniform transnational human resource management policies.

The interviewees areas of work influenced their attitudes. Thus, members of European trade union federations or employers' associations generally have a Europe-centred viewpoint. Often, one side is reproached for having no understanding of the conditions within Europe or the EU, or, conversely, of conditions at national or plant level. This serves to explain a large number of the problems connected with the Europeanisation of industrial relations.

Trade unions generally view European regulations in terms of how they strengthen their capacity to act regardless of whether the individuals or trade unions concerned have a confrontational approach more or are more inclined to follow social partnership strategies. Employers generally view European regulations with more scepticism than trade unions. Industrial relations issues are seen as social matters which are the responsibility of organisations at national level. However, here there is an interesting differentiation. One group (the employers in the metal industry among others) does not consider industrial relations in the narrower sense as a subject for Europeanisation (or only in as far as the matter is forced upon them by the trade unions or by legislation). On the other hand, there are more employers who are more orientated towards social partnership, such as those, for example, in the chemical, construction and food industry, who, with a view to keeping the social peace at least, have a positive view of voluntary European regulations. In countries with a well-established system of co-determination, for example in Germany, there is generally a more open attitude than, for example, in Great Britain, where employers often consider Europeanisation in social political matters as a burden.

The importance of Europeanisation for companies All interviewees reported changes in industrial relations which basically affected all companies - whether global players or medium-sized enterprises. The reasons for this are the growth in the regulatory powers of the EU and changes in competition as a result of the Single Market. The interviewees all agreed, however, that the degree to which companies are affected, depends on the size of the enterprise as well as on the geographic spread of their operations. Big companies who operate in different - European - countries are affected to a greater extent than companies which are only active within individual countries or even only at a regional level. For example, many companies in the Italian food industry only operate in a local protected market.

In addition, specific features of individual industrial sectors are highlighted. The metal and chemical industries are said to be the most internationalised. Here, even medium sized companies operate internationally. In the construction industry, companies are mainly affected by the internationalisation of the labour market with its particular competitive pressures, where working conditions have a special importance. At the same time, many companies in this sector only work in regional markets. Companies in the insurance sector also operate regionally, and are basically integrated into the process of Europeanisation by EU legislation, but there is no significant European competition in this industry.

Interestingly, it was pointed out that the extent to which companies and thus industrial relations are objectively affected by internationalisation is not always reflected in the consciousness of the people active in those companies - whether employees nor the employers. This has its consequences. Although certain problems have taken on a different dimension, the people concerned still act according to their national traditions which, however, deal only partly with the problems Thus, there is a deficit in the political strategic assimilation of economic reality. Partly, this conservative trait in many of the people concerned can be attributed to an uncertainty about the new assimilation patterns. When people begin a journey without knowing the final destination, they prefer to keep to a well-trodden national track, which will lead to a predictable, rather than an optimal outcome.

Partnerships or conflict at the workplace According to the employer association representatives who were interviewed, it is not possible to discern how far increased competition between the different national plants within a company leads to corporatism between workers and the local/national management or rather to more confrontational industrial relations. Numerous concrete examples were given for both patterns of behaviour.

A common feature in all the countries examined is the fact that workplace alliances between unions and management are mainly found in largely internationalised industries, especially in the metal and chemical sectors. The situation in the construction industry is different since there is no competition for investment between sites and not at all within companies - but problems are caused by the international mobility of the workforce.

It is true that trade unions often feel very uncomfortable if they enter into such alliances. National or workplace-based interests carry more weight, though, than international solidarity. However, time and again there seem to be attempts to reach agreements with foreign worker representatives.

In Italy, the confrontational approach of management and unions which was an essential feature of Italian industrial relations for many years, is receding into the background and is being replaced with a more partnership-based approach. However, in Italy, and this is an essential difference from the dualistic German system, it is the mainly the trade union head offices which are involved in such agreements.

The Europeanisation of employee representation at plant level

The general importance of European Works Councils There is no doubt that the European Works Council represents one of the main institutions in the process of the Europeanisation of industrial relations. After more than 20 years of discussion, it was possible to bypass employer opposition, and to enact the directive in September 1994. This had to be transposed into national law by September 1996 at the latest. The benefits of EWC's, though, continue to be a matter of debate. Employers either see EWCs as having no positive function or want to limit them to acting merely as providers of information, while trade unions attribute a much higher importance to EWCs as forms of workers representation.

Employer's assessments of EWCs in different sectors of industry vary considerably. In Germany, representatives of the food and chemical industry welcomed EWC's as an essential means for informing their employees within the framework of the social partnership. In Great Britain a similar view was stated by representatives of the chemical and metal industries. In Germany, however, "Gesamtmetall" - the metal industry employers' association - adopts a sceptical attitude. All employers, regardless of sector or country are of the opinion that EWCs should not be transformed into bodies of co-determination, but should restrict themselves to dealing with information and consultation. French employers have no special objections to EWCs as long as they stick to information and consultation. This is based on the French understanding of consultation which means that worker representatives are given the possibility of commenting on decisions made by the management.

The main reasons for rejecting the EWCs are the costs connected with them and the fact that EWCs cannot cope with different systems of industrial relations.

It is worthy of note that no representative of the employers association or companies at European level had systematically collected information on EWCs. The level of knowledge within employers associations was dependent on trade union research and publications. Whenever they referred to empirical experiences, these were from random reports or their own participation in EWC meetings.

For trade unionists in the individual countries as well as in the European federations, the EWC is a central institution which has an essential role in the Europeanisation of industrial relations as well as in trade union politics as a whole, where, naturally, country specific and historical differences are apparent.

Responses from trade unionists made it clear that they have also yet to make an adequate assessment of their experiences. Accordingly, it is openly stated that work on this must go on. So far, union activity has been clearly focussed on the setting-up of EWCs. The question of what function and what strategic role the EWC should fulfil has been completely neglected. At the moment, trade unions are trying to clarify their future policy within the EU in which EWC's are a central point of reference. There seems to be a certain consensus that in the medium to long-term that EWC's should go beyond merely dealing with information. Here there is support for two kinds of company-level agreements which will, however, clearly not go as far as the collective bargaining/agreements of the German system:

- agreements on soft, exclusively company-related topics
- also agreements on core topics are dealt with, for example, in the employment pact at Volkswagen.

The fear of combine syndicalism is seen as exaggerated and is rather associated with the lack of capacity within the trade unions.

The argument that EWCs should be involved in negotiations is gaining ground among Italian trade unions. Although this reflects the tactical motivations of the Italian trade union movement rather than a strategic view of the consequences of such a move.

For Italian trade unions a key question is their role within EWCs, which emerged as the most controversial item in many EWC meetings. The debate is about the EWC as a source of information in times of continuous change in the corporate structures, since in Italy, there is no such body as a group works council as in Germany or a comité de groupe as in France. That is why it is indisputable that Italian trade unions should participate in EWC meetings. However they have not been successful in pushing this through in many international companies.

The majority of British trade unionists consider EWC's to be an important new element in their strategy. From their point of view, it is essential to develop and use this instrument in the right manner. The EWC is seen as important in several ways: for example to demonstrate the organisational abilities of the trade union, to recruit new members and to receive information on company strategy. British trade unionists stressed, though, that meetings with other employee representatives and the relationships which were thus established were more important than dealings with the employer.

Two of the five British trade unionists were not convinced of the importance of EWC's. For GMB representatives, this was because trade unions had not yet sufficiently thought about the role of EWC's and they were still rather new. For the UCATT representative - a construction industry trade union - it was clear that there was no time or personnel available for EWC work, because of the state of the industry with an enormously decreased membership in the private sector.

Experiences of European Works Councils in practice Information about how EWC's work in practice is limited simply because of the short time they have been in existence. However, trade unionists who have been directly involved in the work of EWCs - mainly as consultants, experts or even members of EWCs - clearly have more practical experiences than the employers. Since the employers' associations do not run EWCs, their knowledge is based on random facts or reports on the workings of EWCs. The trade union experience ranges from EWCs paralysed by conflicts between company representatives over agreements and activities on non-core topics, for example, on the improvement of working conditions, to the organisation of international solidarity during industrial action at individual sites and successfully influencing the investment policy of central management. These experiences demonstrate the broad potential of EWCs and at the same time make clear that the majority of EWCs operate within the framework of their legally assigned tasks. However, there have been some also explicitly negative experiences. Management at Electrolux-Zanussi for example, took advantage of the Italian EWC members in pushing through their local policy.

From the trade union point of view, EWCs have developed into a central element of European co-operation at company level. The interviewees did not know of any international activity involving trade unions or works councils which did no also involve an EWC or at least had the approval of an EWC. If a company does not have an EWC yet, international co-operation is always concentrated on setting one up.

Usually, employers' associations were unaware of the work of, or even the existence of EWCs. The examples mentioned were rather haphazard which is mainly due to the fact that the interviewees had no systematic information to hand. Employers' associations do not have any co-ordinating function like the trade unions. This is because employers do not want to give associations responsibility for this as they consider it to be an internal company matter.

The proposed revision of the European Directive on EWCs The question of whether a revision was envisaged in the original directive is very controversial. UNICE argues that only a review of how the directive works in practice was provided for, and this would not automatically have to result in any changes. Irrespective of this employers' associations are reluctant to see any changes to the directive. The employers' view is that more time should pass, since many companies have not even established EWCs yet. Only in the light of experience, could one decide whether changes are necessary. We also have to take into account that the EWC directive was only enforced in Great Britain in January 2000 when the Labour government ended the British opt-out from social policies.

UNICE announced it would strongly resist any attempt to lower the threshold criteria for the setting up of an EWC. All in all, employers have yet to finalise their position on a possible revision.

At the same time, the question of revision has revealed a particular feature of employers' associations at the European level, which has considerable implications for their ability to act. Thus, the WEM representative pointed out that the formulation of statements on topics where WEM actually has no mandate from its member companies, is a politically sensitive issue. This is another reason why there is no WEM statement on the question of the revision of the EWC directive.

The trade unionists generally supported - to varying degrees - a revision of the directive, even when some thought that it was a little too soon to do so. These doubts were expressed for example, by the representatives of the German trade unions IG Bau, NGG and IG BCE. They stressed that for the time being it was necessary to make use of the full potential of the directive. The IG Metall representative, however, emphasised the inadequacies of the directive, which could only be regarded as a first step towards a form of European worker representation. Even if such doubts were not openly expressed by representatives from other countries, their responses indicated that they were also uncertain about the need for a revision. In Great Britain, for example, the majority supported revision, even though no concrete proposals for changes were made. In Italy, two of the five trade unions had not yet dealt with the topic, although European questions are relatively high on the agenda of these trade unions.

No trade unionist argued for changes aimed at developing the EWC into a German-style co-determination body. Proposals for improvement focussed on what were seen as the deficiencies in the existing directive.

The trade unions' main demands include:

- a clearer definition of information and consultation with the key issues being disclosure of information about future company developments and the right to comment to management before any decisions are finalised;
- the participation of trade unions in EWCs; and
- financial resources for EWCs and the frequency of meetings.

The following suggestions for the revision were made by the European federations:

- the right to training and education;
- regulation of mergers; and
- shortening the setting-up procedure.

There is a continuing debate about lowering the threshold at which companies are required to establish an EWC. At the moment, the limit is

1,000 employees with at least 150 people employed in at least two member states. A lowering of the threshold to 500 employees with at least 100 employees in each country in the whole EU is under discussion. While it is true that this change has been put forward, almost all the interviewees were doubtful whether such an increase in the number of companies eligible to set up an EWC would not hopelessly overburden the limited resources of trade unions especially at European level.

Repercussions on national industrial relations

Interviewees could hardly identify any repercussions for national industrial relations from their own experience of EWCs, not least because of their relatively short experience. Additionally, we have to take into account the fact that the EWC directive has been implemented differently in different countries, that is to say that it was adapted to the terms and conditions of the existing national systems of industrial relations.

In Italy, no repercussions were observed. In other countries, however, there are obvious signs of potential changes. In France, for example, the EWC can replace the combined works council, the comité de groupe.

German trade unionists, for example, referred to the company syndicalist tendencies, which have however, developed independently of EWCs. Another trend, observed by the interviewees, which is definitely gaining momentum, involves major companies in the chemical industry, and also in the food industry increasingly trying to harmonise their human resource management throughout Europe, or at least to co-ordinate it on a European scale. As a result, employees and trade unions are concerned to work towards a greater harmonisation of workers' representation across Europe. It would also be in the management's interest to have a contact at European level in order to resolve controversial questions. In the medium term, EWCs can considerably enhance their importance in such an environment and modify the way the German works council system operates. The conclusion of workplace agreements, which collective bargaining matters could result from this development, particularly as they are common practice in many EU-countries.

In other countries, especially in the UK, the fear of a Euro-syndicalism is seen as typically German, since here - in contrast to Germany - collective bargaining is based at workplace and company levels.

Movement and change are, however, also evident in the UK: here one can observe that the EWC leads to a debate about representative structures above workplace level. This was backed up by representatives from the AEEU and the TGWU. According to their statements, the setting-up of

EWCs has simultaneously led to the establishment of new national structures of worker representation.

Representatives from the European trade union federations referred in particular to changes in other countries. Many interviewees pointed out that in countries where the competition between politically orientated trade unions has been dominant, the EWC often forced competing trade unions to agree on joint representation, since the number of EWC seats is often smaller than the number of competing trade unions. This could lead to new forms of co-operation - especially in France and Italy.

The employers' representatives saw EWCs as having hardly any repercussions on national industrial relations. They repeatedly emphasised in their answers, however, that they had scarcely any information about EWCs. In the UK, the employers' associations also partly saw the necessity to think over the structures of national worker representation.

Effects on international co-operation between employer associations and union federations

EWCs have had no impact on co-operation between employers' associations. Only the representatives of EEF in the UK reported a that international co-operation had been attempted. All attempts at processing information, providing guidance or co-ordinating EWCs by, for example, the association of the European metal industry employers or by the European federation of construction industry employers, were rejected as interference in the internal company affairs. The question of worker representation at plant level is mainly considered to be a socio-political matter. According to the majority of employers' associations these questions should not be the subject of European regulations. That is why it is argued that this is not the responsibility of the European federations. Only UNICE has a mandate to discuss socio-political questions. The trade unions are of the opinion however, that UNICE uses this right mainly in order to avoid socio-political guidelines etc.

In contrast, trade union co-operation has been considerably strengthened according to the German and British trade unionists. The importance of European trade union federations has been considerably enhanced through their support in the setting-up EWCs as well as through co-ordination of EWC work in practice. Meanwhile, many federations and most of the German individual trade unions have guidelines on EWCs. Combined consultants are in most cases full-time trade union officers from the country where the enterprise has its head office and their task is to keep in contact with their counterparts in other countries. At the level of the European federations, there are now different kinds of bodies which bring together national trade union officials who are responsible for EWCs. They hold regular meetings to exchange experiences, to discuss problems and to co-ordinate their demands. Bilateral contacts between trade unions of different countries have been strengthened along with co-operation in different companies. Finally, considerably more trade unionists and worker representatives are involved in European co-operation than used to be the case. The EWCs have clearly contributed to a development where international contacts are no longer restricted to "Trade union diplomats". Over the medium term this will have a considerable impact on the outlook of trade union representatives and some change is already perceptible.

European union federations have played a leading role in the course of establishing of EWCs in many companies. The European trade union federations have become a trade union protagonist with a recognised autonomy. Negotiations to set up EWCs were partly led by the European federations or they were actively involved in them. The European federations are indispensable for co-ordinating existing EWCs. This increase in importance exposes the limited resources available to the European federations. There has been an increase in network structures in response to this and this is leading - slowly - to a division of labour between national trade unions and European federations.

In France, European matters are given a low priority. National problems are still the focus of trade union activity and this is partly due to the extremely low levels of membership, especially in private industry. Another factor is the significant role played by the French government in industrial relations, as, for example, in the attempt to introduce a 35-hour week.

In Italy, too, national factors play a key role. Co-operation between the competing national trade unions is often necessary as the large number of foreign enterprises and the limited number of seats for Italian representatives means that it is often the case that one trade unionist within a EWC represents all three organisations. At the moment, there are, however, still cases where no Italian representatives turn up at the EWC meeting because they have not yet been nominated because of a lack of agreement between the three organisations.

A greater degree of international co-operation only develops where there are concrete trade union interests as in the case of the chemicals industry.

Connections with the respective European federations continue to be weak or non-existent. It is only in the food industry that the European trade union structure is recognised as having an important co-ordinating role.

Against this background, the chemicals industry is the one sector where closer and more frequent contacts are apparently being established and fostered among southern European countries (Italy, France and Spain). The trade unions explain this with the phrase "different models". However, there is more to it: these closer and more frequent contacts do not take place solely between trade unions involve employers' associations. They come together in quite a structured "forum" ("trilateral") which meets regularly at least twice a year. The reasons for this development are thought to be:

- the similar structure of industry in each country - based on SMEs;
- the similar "politically aligned and not company-centred" trade union culture.

Industrial relations have so far remained in the background ('We keep each other informed about developments'), and they work together over issues which do not imply any conflicts, (for example a joint EU-financed programme on further vocational training with final international conference in May 1999).

It is striking that the German trade union and the German employers' association were excluded or did not take part. It should be noted that the "forum" is closely tied to the structure of the industry where the German trade union is particularly predominant: 'There is the fear that the German predominance which is typical for this sector of industry might reproduce itself within the forum. On the other hand, one is aware of the fact that the initiative might have little impact without the Germans.'

Nevertheless, this is certainly an important development: instead of seeking co-operation or conciliation through the European federation, a coalition between weaker participants seems to be favoured. The result, in the sense of greater co-operation at European level, is clear.

The Europeanisation of co-determination at company level

European decision makers have been trying for years to develop and to establish a legal basis for joint-stock companies operating in more than one European country. This attempt is based on the view that completion of the European Single Market should go hand in hand with the creation of European company law in order to harmonise competition between enterprises in the different member states and in order to minimise distortions. A general harmonisation of national laws is currently considered to be impossible, therefore the aim, as a first step, is to create a European level framework for companies operating internationally. On the one hand, this should standardise the fiscal treatment of international companies which, at the moment, is regulated by a complicated pattern of bi- and multi-lateral double taxation agreements. On the other hand, questions of co-determination at company level should be regulated by the European directive for such European enterprises.

The development of such a directive has up to now been blocked by a number of obstacles. In 1996 negotiations had come to another standstill, the Commission appointed a group of high-ranking experts (named the Davignon group after its chairman) whose task it was to find a way out of the deadlock. The directive which emerged from the proposals made by the Davignon group, is similar to the EWC directive in its legal methods.

> Given the need for agreement at European level, the closed system of legally defined co-determination rights is increasingly being replaced with more open procedures and minimum requirements. This approach leads away from the restrictive legislation which limits the possibilities for action of the people concerned in the companies, towards more open procedures (Höland, 1998, p. 64).

The most important and controversial points about co-determination concern the circumstances in which a European Company (SE) can be established and, given the vast differences between the member states, defines which co-determination/participation regulations apply. From a German point of view in order to avoid a 'flight away from co-determination by re-structuring', there is now a provision saying that an SE may only be founded when setting up a holding company, a joint subsidiary or in a merger, and not used to re-structure the legal form of a company. The co-determination regulations should be negotiated by the parties involved. If no agreement is reached in these bodies, a subsidiary rule comes into force. With regard to the German legislation, this would mean some cuts. It is true, that the subsidiary rule provides for worker representatives to be members of the supervisory board, but the number of seats should only be 20% as a minimum. Opinions on the envisaged directive are very varied. Höland, for example, despite all the shortcomings of the planned regulation draws the following conclusion:

> However, the danger of an erosion of the German system of co-determination is higher in a Europe with absolutely no co-determination regulations than with a version of a "light" SE, which contains a requirement on co-determination below or equivalent to that of the German supervisory board, but which at least establishes limits below which one must not go (Höland, 1998, p. 65).

Given the shortcomings of the directive from a trade union point of view, IG Metall draws a different conclusion:

> For IG Metall, the present proposals are not suitable to provide for co-determination at a European level and at the same time to safeguard the German system of co-determination which has been developed over decades and which we judge to be a cornerstone of our system of industrial relations (Benz-Overhage, 1999, p. 2).

The directive could not be passed and has been put on hold because of among other things, a vote of the Spanish government (which was, however, motivated by other aims).

The interviews with association representatives revealed that trade unions and employers no longer attach any special importance to negotiations over the European Company directive.

The main interest of German trade unions in the envisaged European Company statute was in the regulation of co-determination at company level. After it became apparent that German co-determination rights would be maintained, this interest faded away. IG BCE as well as IG Metall assumed that the German model of co-determination could be promoted through the relevant European Company regulations.

Non-German trade unions place an even lower value on the importance of the European Company since the central concern of the trade unions has clearly been met, i.e. that the respective national systems of co-determination remain. Here, we have to consider that, depending on how the European directive is drawn up, Germany is threatened with far-reaching cuts in co-determination rights. But in many other member states, there are hardly any legal rights to co-determination at company level and so they are not in danger of being undermined by European law - quite the reverse.

The situation for employers looks very different: German employers are looking at two aspects of the European Company. On the one hand, the associations aim to balance out the "competitive disadvantage of German co-determination". The chemical industry representative was of the opposite view. For him, central to the considerations on co-determination was the idea of spreading the advantages of the German system of co-determination. On the other hand, there are questions of tax legislation. At the time of the interviews (1998/99), all interviewees said they were dissatisfied with the compromise which is seen as a missed opportunity. However, the topic is no longer seen as being of major importance.

The responses from the European employers' representatives reflect the division of responsibilities between the employers' associations. The sectoral associations have mainly dealt with the tax legislation questions since co-determination at company level was considered to be a social matter and thus the responsibility of UNICE.

In Italy, the responses focussed on the rejection of the German model of co-determination.

In the UK, the discussion moved away from inter-company co-determination according to the German pattern (which anyway is seen as simply not on the agenda) towards the idea of workplace-based body for information purposes which had been planned by the Commission but rejected by the employers.

Summarised results at workplace and company level

With the above strategic discussion as a starting point we summarise how far the interviewed experts want to defend their own national institutions and procedures and to what extent they want to see a shift of regulation powers to the European level. Here, the following questions are of special interest:

What strategic importance is attached to EWCs?

In all the countries examined, the employers' associations do not generally attach far-reaching importance to the EWCs. In particular, they are not seen as central to a Europeanisation of industrial relations - in the sense of an extension of regulatory powers at the European level. They are either considered to be altogether superfluous or their importance is limited to being merely a transmission belt for information in order to get employees to endorse the corporate strategy.

The views of trade unions are completely different. EWCs are generally seen as an essential instrument to reinforce transnational trade union co-operations. The starting point are weaknesses in the regulatory framework of national systems of industrial relations at company level. These weaknesses should be compensated for at European level. There are, however, considerable differences between different countries as to how the reinforcement of international co-operation within the framework of EWCs should be organised.

At the same time, the political perspective of EWCs is not limited to a specific company. They are seen rather as an essential starting point in establishing a European perspective in every-day trade union activities. A concrete future role for EWCs is a controversial issue. So far, the trade unions have dealt exclusively with setting-up EWCs in as many enterprises as possible. All interviewees agreed that EWCs should in future be carefully built on and upgraded. Wherever workplace agreements were already part of everyday collective bargaining, the possibility of concluding workplace agreements by the EWCs was welcomed.

What experiences have there been so far in EWC work and how can they be evaluated?

Concrete experiences of the work of the EWCs are in contrast with the importance attached to them. It is true that there are many examples where the existence of EWCs has proved to be useful from a union point of view for solving plant and company related problems. There are, however, also plenty of negative experiences and many well-known difficulties associated with international co-operation. This is revealed, for example, in the sluggish process of setting up new EWCs according to paragraph 6 (since September 1996), which almost all interviewees reported on.

In all only 540 agreements had been concluded by October 1999 - thus only about one third of the companies covered by EWC legislation actually have one. Often, not even a special negotiating body has been set up. Besides the usual obstacles in transnational worker representation - for example the competition between different workplaces - the difficulties of international and, above all, of intercultural co-operation are shown to be very significant. The existence of different systems of industrial relations and thus different traditions and cultural orientations as well as, not least, communication problems, due to lack of language knowledge, indicate that a longer learning process is needed before EWCs can take on the more comprehensive functions of company level worker representation. Against this background EWCs can only become relevant when they are embedded in national systems of worker representation and build their strength from there.

It is evident that national industrial relations still predominate in all countries, even where enterprises are heavily internationalised or Europeanised.

What repercussions are there on national industrial relations?

The first signs of repercussions of EWCs on national industrial relations can be observed in the personal orientation of the participants. Here, the EWC is more important for the trade union side than for the employers. However, in the opinion of one person we spoke to, repercussions on the structure of national industrial relations are evident but yet limited. This tendency might even be reinforced in the future if EWCs manage to establish themselves as institutions and grow in number.

How is the envisaged Europeanisation of co-determination at company level assessed?

The protection of national vested rights clearly dominates the debate about the European Company statute. Here, we have to take into account that only Germany among the countries examined is in danger of having to accept major weakening of the co-determination rights at company level. That is why debates on the EWCs have considerably less importance in France, Italy and the UK than in Germany. The responses of the German experts indicate that industrial relations elements in the envisaged European directive were only worthy of attention as long as this danger - which some employers also understand to be a opportunity - existed. After the German company level co-determination (board) had been given appropriate consideration (in the draft), German interest also declined relatively quickly.

The relationship between the protection of national vested rights and an extension of European regulations

On the whole, the discussions with experts show that we have to consider very carefully what we understand by the term Europeanisation of industrial relations or by a European social model at plant and company level. Neither positions presented at the beginning of the chapter (re-nationalisation or supplanting of national industrial relations by European ones) seem to describe the process of Europeanisation sufficiently. This process does not take place as an alternative development between two poles, but as a contradictory process involving national safeguards and the simultaneous development of a European regulatory framework. This dialectical process is interwoven with the different or even opposing interests of employees and trade unions on the one side and enterprises and employers on the other. At the same time, differences become apparent within the trade unions' as well as in the employers' camp in the different countries, for example along sectoral lines. The contradictory development of industrial relations can only be understood after analysing the concrete interests. Basically, a situation has emerged whereby employers oppose European regulations. Behind this is the calculation that under the conditions of a free economic Single Market the retention of national systems industrial relations provides them with a competitive advantage. This, in turn, puts pressure on trade unions to make concessions.

From the trade union perspective there is a contradictory and inconsistent response. This reaction includes demands for the enforcement of European regulations as well as national protection of vested rights. If we look closer at this, it turns out not to be a strategic mistake. Trade unions cannot ask abstractly for the best possible level of regulation for the different areas of industrial relations in the abstract. They have to take into account their prevailing relative strengths and the framework conditions. To clarify: the trade union line of action is not based on an ideal or a well-considered strategy, but involves adapting to realities. This was developed at a critical stage and shows many weaknesses. These, however, cannot be defined with the assumed contrast between national protection of actual vested rights and an extension of European regulations.

The development of trade unions and employers' associations

The importance and function of trade unions and employers' associations in Europe

In a paper, mentioned above, on the position of trade unions between national states and European Union, Wolfgang Streeck (1998, p. 10) recently claimed that there has been a re-orientation of the strategic approach towards a Europe-related policy particularly by German trade unions. Here, he is not mainly talking about a reinforcing through the trade unions' ability to act at European level in strengthening of the European associations, as is emphasised, for example, by Hoffmann (1997a and 1997b).[4] A European trade union policy should take the "principle of subsidiarity" of the European Union into account and thus start from the respective national circumstances and have a different form in each country. This line of argument has consequences for the entire field of trade union policy on Europe,[5] but also for the development and function of trade union organisations themselves, which has to be dealt with in this context. Thus, the 'further development the European contexts of national organisations' trade union policy' (Streeck, 1998, p. 10) is of predominant importance. On the other hand, employers' organisations are also confronted with the consequences of the process of European integration as a reference point and framework for their work. There is, however,

---

[4] Yet Hoffmann does not simply support strengthening European trade union structures by increasing the financial and personnel resources but claims that Europe has to become an integral part of trade union action at national level(Hoffmann, 1997, p. 6) Similar claims are made by Rath (1991, p. 236) that trade union members at company and regional level should be in a position to 'consider the European dimension of their work and to act accordingly'.
[5] A general overview on the problems of trade unions in Europe can be found in Waddington (1997). For a comparative analysis of different national orientations also cf. Hyman (1996).

according to several references in the literature, an enormous discrepancy in the personnel, material and organisational resources between employees' and employers' associations, which is to the disadvantage of the trade unions (Platzer, 1991, pp.184-86; Kohler-Koch, 1996, pp. 195 f.).

Against this general background and on the basis of our experts' interviews with representatives of selected associations, we want to consider the following questions, in order to obtain more exact information on the practical experience of the associations in the process of the European integration:

- What levels of the associations deal with the development of industrial relations in Europe and how are these levels co-ordinated?
- What structural weaknesses and potential for development currently exist in relations between the national and European organisations? What functions should the European and national federations fulfil?
- What problems are there in the communication between the associations of different countries as well as between national associations and the European federations?
- And lastly: what similarities and what differences are there with regard to the views on the tasks and functions of associations between the national (here: German) associations and the European federations on the one hand, and between trade unions and employers' associations on the other hand?

The organisational structure adopted by trade unions and employers' associations to deal with the issue of Europe

In essence, we could support the hypothesis that employers' associations resist the formation of European institutions or rules in industrial relations, possibly because they hope for better results from collective bargaining and workplace disputes if international competitive pressures are at work. For the trade unions, however, the key issues are re-gaining the ability to act and to design. These controversial views are basically also reflected in the way the question of "Europe" is integrated into the respective associations where we can, however, to some extent find major differences between the individual trade unions and the employers' associations, as was revealed in our experts' interviews. In interpreting the answers, we have to take into account the different situations of each association in terms of its role in industrial relations in each country.

The organisational structures as well as the extent to which the issue of "Europe" is discussed are completely different in German trade unions. Despite some detailed differences, we can state that in all five trade unions in which we did interviews, the European issues are dealt with across departments. In contrast to the employers' associations, unions also deal with the narrower issue of "Industrial Relations in Europe" across different sectors- which is another reflection of the significantly higher importance unions give to Europe-related questions in comparison to the employers' associations. Yet, there are major differences between the German trade unions in this area, for example, the EWC work is organised in a project form by IG Metall,[6] whereas IG BCE has a "European relations" department, etc. We do not want to go into any more detail on this. None of the trade unions however, completely centralise "European relations". They tend to be dealt with in some kind of matrix. Overall, we can state that German trade unions already attach considerable importance to European issues and especially, to industrial relations matters, which are dealt with through a well-established or at least a developing structure. However, we have the impression that there is still a tendency to leave "European issues" to the specialists.

A different picture emerges in Italy. Within trade unions, European questions are dealt with within the traditional structures. The international department has responsibility and/or there is an EWC officer. They often do no more than pay lip service to European issues. This is also reflected in weaknesses in trade union educational work, in terms of both quantity and quality.

British trade unions have built up complex and qualitatively different structures for dealing with European questions. The GMB is the only trade union among those interviewed, which has established an office in Brussels. The AEEU and TGWU also dedicate considerable funds to European work. Five out of the six trade unions, AEEU, GMB, TGWU GPMU and UNIFI have specialists on Europe. They also stress, however, that they try not to deal with European questions as topics only for experts. The fact that three out of five trade unions are not industry-specific but general (occupational) trade unions results in different officers dealing directly with European questions and having leading roles in different European federations. However, British trade unionists also expressed the fear that many European matters often remain within a small circle and are not conveyed to the members. The British union federation, the TUC, has established a "National Contact Point" on European questions which

---

[6] Cf. the overview in the handbook for European Works Councils (Project European Works Councils at IG Metall, 1997, pp. 8f.).

regularly assembles experts on European matters from its member trade unions.

The French trade unions attach very little importance to European matters. The focus of trade union activity remains at the national level. The reason for this can be found in the French trade unions' membership problems. The French trade union movement is at the crossroads: given its weakness and the desperate state of membership organisation it has to tackle the question with whatever means are available to ensure its survival, renewal and further development. Here, several hypotheses can be formulated which don't correspond to the strategies of specific trade union organisations but which point towards a basic approach or possibilities for action influenced by economic factors. The CGT is going through an important internal process of renewal which the CFDT tackled several years ago. The CGT-FO is also involved in a complicated internal discussion process which is being keenly observed by the media. All this explains why European questions have a very low priority for French trade unions.

Employers' associations are based on national structures to an even greater extent than the trade unions. The following view, expressed in one of our interviews with the experts, seems to be valid for the German employers along these lines: 'In general, the associations have not been considering Europeanisation and internationalisation for long enough, although business relations have been for a long time', with some variations.

Thus European issues are dealt with differently in the associations: Within smaller associations they are the responsibilities of general managers since their roles embrace almost all tasks. Within bigger associations, there are basically two alternatives: either there is a department of International/European relations, as is the case with Gesamtmetall or, as in most cases, it is an inter-departmental issue with the area of industrial and social relations included in the department "Collective bargaining and social policy" or similar departments. Generally, questions of industrial relations in Europe have a rather low priority in German employers' associations.

Awareness of increasing European co-operation and the establishment of corresponding structures is growing with Italian employers. Efforts made by the chemicals industry have concentrated on setting-up bilateral transnational co-operation. Employers in the metal industry are complaining about the lack of activities within the national employers' association, Confindustria, and are aiming at improving the co-ordination with the metal industry employers in other countries.

The British employers' associations are very sceptical about the Europeanisation of association structures. First, they repeatedly stressed that there were companies' rather than employers' associations at European level. Above all, the fear was expressed that socio-political initiatives from the EU commission could strengthen the European associations to the disadvantage of the national ones. The responsibility for social questions is in most cases assigned to UNICE and not to the industrial associations.

European matters represent the central task of European employers' (companies') associations. They have, however, very few staff. WEM, the employers' association in the west-European metal industry, for example, consists of only a head, an assistant and a secretary. There is no association at all in the food and luxury goods industry, just a policy co-ordinator which the employers follow with regard to the trade unions in the food and beverages industry.[7]

This demonstrates how unimportant the European federations appear to the national employers' associations and also the companies themselves. The national member associations value their autonomy highly. Furthermore, there is a far-reaching division of labour with UNICE in, for example, the metal industry. First of all, the responsibility of UNICE is assumed. Only if the metal industry is exclusively affected does WEM become active on its own. Otherwise, WEM as well as the national member organisations influence the policy of UNICE.

UNICE currently employs a total of 35 staff and it is the most important European association with regard to industrial relations.[8] However, even here it is obvious that the employers attach little importance to their European organisations in comparison to the trade unions. There is a regular exchange of views on different questions but no co-ordination of issues in the same way as unions deal with EWCs for example. Statutory meetings are often prepared by working groups and experts are invited from the member associations. They always follow the same pattern. The views of the different members form the starting point. These are discussed and, if possible, are condensed to a joint position.

Overall, in terms of industrial relations, we can state that association structures at the European level are inadequate for making binding agreements. On the one hand, this is due to the very heterogeneous structure of the existing associations. Within UNICE, for instance, the types of member association vary considerably (Rath, 1991, pp. 282 f.; Platzer, 1991, p. 186). On the other hand, there is political opposition to

---

[7] A more detailed description of the organisation of associations at European level can be found in Platzer (1991, pp. 184 - 89).
[8] For details on UNICE see Platzer (1991, pp. 186f.).

this as not only the national associations and especially the employers themselves insist on their autonomy.

A third reason is the fact that the national associations have very different functions in the framework of industrial relations in each country so it is necessary to agree on the smallest common denominator at European level. Trade unions have a similar problem but a different solution.

Co-operation and division of labour between national and European trade union and employers' associations

The question of co-operation and division of labour between associations at national and European level has been mentioned several times in the previous section. In this context, we were more interested in what measures have been taken to improve co-operation between trade unions in different countries.

According to our findings there are numerous activities within the European federation, which, despite some differences, are very similar. In addition to the tasks related to EWCs, these include:

- organisation and co-ordination of Social Dialogue for industrial sectors and co-ordination of the trade unions involved;
- meetings, conferences, training for EWCs and industrial sectors - in this context information about working arrangements in other countries is sometimes imparted;
- data collection and distribution about industrial relations developments; and
- studies on selected topics, for instance, on European collective bargaining.[9]

From the point of view of the experts interviewed, there is also, despite satisfaction with the work of the Eurofederations, criticism of the division of responsibilities between the European trade union federations and the national trade unions. Their main conclusion was that there is a general situation of change. In the mid-80s, the federations were founded as EU lobbyists. They had to be transformed into strong organisations with a primary responsibility to organise the flow of information between national trade unions across Europe in order to avoid the present laborious process of bilateral exchanges of information. This has led to a considerable change to structures and to the responsibilities of the people involved. It was not

---

[9] Cf. Baumann, Laux and Schnepf (1997).

always easy to cope with this problem and there was not always a satisfactory outcome.

On the whole, the opinions of German trade unions and the problems mentioned were common to the Eurofederations, but with some surprising shifts in emphasis.

Thus, there were often complaints about inadequate financial and personnel resources, as, for example, at the EMF, which not only criticised the level of resources but also remarked: this has resulted in the European federation being dependent on the EU, especially in financial matters, which is not good for trade union autonomy.

The EFBWW takes a different view: the exchange of information takes place through statutory bodies and has been considerably reinforced over the last few years. An increase in personnel and financial resources of the EFBWW is not considered to be important at all for further improvements and certainly not the first priority. It is much more important for the national trade unions to integrate European issues, problems and views naturally into their work and restructure their work accordingly. The starting point is the division of specialist responsibilities within the trade unions which make it difficult for the EFBWW to get information about the situations in each country. Additionally, the national trade unions need to take the initiative and supply information in order to support the lobby work of the EFBWW.

A final key issue was similarly discussed by representatives of some other associations: the focus of trade union work is the company. This can only be adequately dealt with by the national organisations. That is why national organisations are decisive on questions of working conditions and pay. It would, however, make sense if the *transfer* of information and the co-ordination of important matters were improved and made more efficient. Here, the national organisations, too, need to consider changes, an essential issue being to overcome divisions in trade unions. This is not, however, a question of the division of responsibilities between European and national levels or the lack of a formal transfer of sovereignty.

The attitude of the UK trade unions towards the European federations is completely different. Bearing in mind, that three of the trade unions interviewed are general unions and thus belong to several European federations: the AEEU belongs to five federations, the GMB to seven, and the TGWU to nine. Only UNIFI, UCATT and GPMU are affiliated to just one federation.

Some trade unions expressed strong criticism of the federations. In one case, a Euro-federation was even reproached for not being interested in providing real benefits for the affiliated organisations. They concentrated more on making a name for themselves, which impeded the work of the national trade unions. Other opinions were split and several interviewees stressed that there are important differences between the European federations. Whilst some work mainly as lobbyists, there are others, such as the textile and garment federation, which are able to sign agreements with employers.

The comments made by the AEEU and TGWU were focussed on the EMF. The AEEU sees the EMF as facing a decision as to whether it can develop its policies autonomously or be bound by the instructions of the affiliated organisations. The AEEU pleads for a greater autonomy, but not all EMF members share this view. For the TGWU, the EMF would operate as a European trade union, if the political will existed.

Unfortunately, for the French trade unions, the European federations are often only an outlet for their political differences. A prime example of this was the question of admission of the CGT into the ETUC, which was blocked by the CGT-FO. On the other hand, European trade union politics can provide the impetus for a better co-operation between the French trade unions.

On the whole, in comparing national and European associations, it seems remarkable that the latter, on the basis of their own specific situation, do not seem to be aiming at reinforcing their position at the expense of the national associations. Instead, they tend to emphasise the value of the national associations. In our view this does not just demonstrate their dependency but also possibly an understanding of the Europeanisation of industrial relations as a multi-level process in which national systems will continue to have a greater importance.

Employers' associations have a rather heterogeneous structure in the countries examined. We can differentiate them into:

- Economic (enterprises') associations,
- Socio-political (employers') associations,
- Mixed forms of organisations of the two above,
- Informal co-operation or contacts.

Formally, UNICE in Brussels deals in most cases with socio-political affairs, while the usually more important economic associations deal with other matters - especially lobby work at the Commission. By and large, the associations expressed their satisfaction with the work of the European organisations, which may also partly reflect their relatively low-level demands in this respect. The most important task of the European associations, in terms of content, is considered to be the procuring and distributing of technical information. Alongside the formal activities of co-ordination and communication, the European employers' organisations are a focus for informal contacts. Direct bi-national contacts independent of the European organisations' hardly seem to exist.

As a general impression, we can state that the German employers' associations attach considerably less importance to the European employers' associations than to the trade unions. In contrast to the latter, European questions are dealt with much more forcefully inside the companies themselves.

While the national employers' representatives mostly expressed satisfaction with the division of responsibilities between national and European organisations, the assessments of European representatives were often completely different. One employers' association, for instance, complained that the exchange of information was very bad. Information produced by them was often disregarded. Altogether the national associations did not seem to see any sense in establishing a European structure analogous to the trade union one. A more moderate statement was made by another association: the exchange of information worked quite well, even if improvements were possible. It was, however, feared that agreement on European perspectives would be understood by the trade unions as a concession to negotiate minimum standards. That is why many national associations shy away from official European agreements and want to see a guarantee that the European associations do not become the employers' contact person for the Commission or for other bodies.

UNICE, too, is dependent to a great extent on its member associations, and through these on the member companies. It does not have a mandate autonomously but is attributed with one in an ad-hoc manner if the member associations have decided on it.

An explanation for these apparent differences in the perception between German and European employers' associations appear to us to be mainly due to the specific positions of the different camps. The national associations, wherever possible, do not want to share any responsibilities, especially since they see the European association structures as having a limited importance. The latter would like to broaden their competence, firstly in their own interest and secondly because European matters have a much higher importance from their perspective. However, compared to the national associations, they are in a much weaker position, since they are not independent.

The complex relationships between national and European structures of trade unions and employers' associations

In conclusion, there is a dichotomy between national and European organisation which determines the structure for the employers' associations. The situation does not vary much in the countries examined. Generally, the national associations insist on their autonomy. The background to this is the preference of their member companies to tackle their European affairs principally by themselves and to reduce European activities to mainly lobbying.

With trade unions, this dichotomy is, at least in Germany and Great Britain, becoming less apparent. It is true that national organisation levels are still dominant, but slowly, and in a contradictory way, a division of labour is emerging between them. This results from an understanding that a combination of the two levels of organisation means more scope for solving problems. At present, the trade unions are faced with the task of reforming their national structures as well as the European framework, since the existing structures and patterns of behaviour are obviously no longer sufficient to deal with the many new responsibilities.

The French and Italian trade unions remain, however, much more nationally orientated. Despite the enthusiastic rhetoric on Europe, basic changes of practice are still needed.

Europeanisation or re-nationalisation of collective bargaining

The importance and role of collective bargaining systems in Europe

Collective bargaining policy is a central element of industrial relations. It can involve both compromise and conflict and has faced the need to adapt through the period of industrialisation. Never before, though, has the need to change been so serious as in the current period of globalisation and Europeanisation and the shift in focus to the company level.

With the introduction of the Euro, collective bargaining has suddenly become a key influence on the monetary policy of the European Central Bank in Frankfurt/Main. For example in Germany until 1999, with the yearly expert reports of the "five wise men", people were used to debating about the pros and cons of a collective bargaining policy, especially wage policy aimed at economic stability. This led to arguments between advocates of supply-side and demand-orientated economic policies. However, today people can no longer take part in this debate. The whole thing has been removed to the European level (at least in the Euro zone). Wage policy has taken on the role of the adjustment variable with the abolition of fluctuating exchange rates. Thus, a study carried out by the Wissenschaftszentrum Berlin (Berlin Research Centre) argues that, if negotiators from both sides of industry in Germany do not fully take into account the influence on European inflation or agree high pay rises, then

European inflation will rise and the ECB will implement a deflationary policy. A competition-orientated wage policy would thus be in the interest of the two sides of industry, according to the study; as it keeps inflation low and does not lead the ECB to restrictive counter-measures resulting in an increase in unemployment (Kasten and Soskice, 1999, p. 21).

As it is well-known that German trade unions take a different view we do not have to go into more detail. They argue that a moderate wage policy encourages "beggar-my-neighbour" strategy and collective bargaining, which, by consciously not making full use of the national room for manoeuvre, aims at improving one's own competitive position at the expense of neighbouring countries in Europe (Schulten, 1999, p. 1). Trade unions are trying to avoid undercutting each other by making the first steps in establishing a European collective bargaining relation policy.

Both views of collective bargaining policy have shifted their focus towards Europe. It is important, though, to see the nuances, i.e. the actual direction and pace of these changes. There are, for instance, suggestions about the increase of the basic social protection, the fixing of minimum standards as well as defining a lower limit for the total social expenses of a country with reference to the per-capita gross national product (Lecher, 1999, p. 339). Schulten considers the co-ordination approach to be realistic, and achievable over the medium term: joint collective bargaining targets could be formulated within the European (industrial) trade unions which would then be put into practice in the different conditions of each system of collective bargaining. One advantage of proceeding in this way would be limited competition between national regimes without the immediate need for setting-up a supra-national collective bargaining system. It is thus a medium-term strategy which keeps all essential future options open. Some small concrete steps have directly been taken in this direction (Lecher, 1999, p. 342): For example some national collective agreements (Belgium and Netherlands) refer to collective regulations in other countries - especially in Germany.[10] Furthermore, the Belgian trade unions and the North-Rhine Westphalia collective bargaining district of IG Metall have agreed to participate in collective bargaining negotiations (collective bargaining commissions and negotiation body in Germany). At the third collective bargaining policy conference of the European Metalworkers federation, it was decided to co-ordinate the terms of collective agreements in Europe. Additionally, the "Collective Bargaining Policy" department of IG Metall in Frankfurt/Main decided that their regional offices should

---

[10] It goes without saying that this can be interpreted the other way round: In order to secure the edge of the so-called Dutch "Polder model" - and exactly opposite to Germany -in the future, the Netherlands, for example, are thus entering into a regime competition.

inform them in future about developments in neighbouring countries and possibly co-ordinate certain activities, for example "Küste" (coast) the regional office with Scandinavia, Bavaria with Austria and the Czech Republic etc. A decision at the 9th congress of the European Trade Union Confederation in Helsinki in July 1999 stresses the need to co-ordinate collective bargaining policies in the individual countries. This decision also lists the possible areas to be included: education and training, health and safety, working conditions and equal opportunities) (ETUC, 1999, pp. 3f.).

However - according to Jacobi - there already is, although little noticed, the outline of a European wage area, even if it is uncoordinated and does not look exactly as the trade unions imagine it: collective agreements at a national level show a surprisingly high degree of convergence; wage increases only compensate for losses in purchasing power, productivity growth remains excluded, and there is no compensation for reductions in income through higher taxes and/or contributions to social insurance. There is a widespread re-distribution of income taking place to the advantage of company profits (Jacobi, 1997, p. 55).

In the context of the Europeanisation of collective bargaining policy, a striking fact is the weakness of the European employers' associations. This means that the second partner for the negotiation and settlement of agreements is often lacking. Thus is the corresponding European federation to the EFBWW, for example, the European employers' organisation for the construction industry, FIEC. FIEC, however, does not fully represent the national employers' organisations. Some are members of other umbrella associations, such as, for example, the "European Builders". Furthermore, the claim of the European employers' associations to be representative is limited by the potential for national employers' associations, companies themselves and "independent" lobbyists in Brussels to exert their influence (Baumann, Laux and Schnepf, 1997, p. 141).

However, the question remains how long European employers'/ enterprises' associations can afford to sit back. Their strategy - to ensure the lowest possible degree of regulation of working conditions in Europe - has so far been relatively successful. But the potential price of taking a back seat and the deliberate weakness of their employers' European institutions means they risk losing their role as leading opinion formers in industrial relations.

These considerations form the framework in which we asked representatives of trade unions and employers' associations at national and European level about:

- their knowledge of the collective bargaining systems and the collective bargaining policies of sister organisation/member associations in other countries as influences on their own policies;

- the increase in importance now and in future of co-ordination of collective bargaining policy in Europe and the forms in which this will happen;
- their opinion on collective bargaining at European level and the possible areas of regulation;
- the effects of the EURO on the collective bargaining systems and the extent to which associations were prepared for this.

The knowledge of collective bargaining systems in the different countries as a reference point for action

The answers reveal an interesting constellation which is more than a mere reflection of the different situations and roles: Whereas national associations - trade unions and employers - define their knowledge as not sufficient, there are complaints at European level, that the information on collective bargaining produced is only inadequately used or the co-operation for the collection of information is insufficient on the side of the national associations. This, however, is where the similarities between the social partners end.

The German trade union representatives, for example, personally feel that their knowledge is not yet sufficient. This is, however, not perceived as a special shortcoming, if the deficits are compensated in three ways:

- by the establishment of a reasonable matrix organisation, which makes it possible to ask further questions in other departments (e.g. collective bargaining),
- by the establishment of a good personal network of the full-time union officers from foreign sister organisations to retrieve necessary information via this network when needed,
- by leaving this task partly to the Euro-federations.

The situation looks similar in the Italian and British trade unions. The knowledge about the other systems is limited. The European Trades Union Confederation serves as a source of information, but also other sources, such as, for example EIRO, the ordinary press and research institutes. In general, it was revealed that the flow of information between the European federation and the national trade unions is not always free of problems. The representative of the British GMB, for instance, did not know much about the work of the EMF in Brussels.

Knowledge about the collective bargaining landscape in different European countries is a matter of course for the European trade unionists. As far as the European Trade Union Confederation (ETUC) is concerned, its executive committee publishes a yearly report, based among other things on the work of the European Trade Union Institute (ETUI). However, this information often remains, according to the impression of the ETUC, in the board departments of the national trade unions. The Euro-Federation FIET organises a regular exchange of information (yearly reports on collective bargaining movements, annual meetings offer possibilities for exchange). How far they are actually used could, however, not be clarified in more detail by the interviews.

Let us now move on to the employers' associations, and here, first of all to Germany: with the exception of "Gesamtmetall" (this association is very well organised with regard to information policy) and the construction industry/business (on the basis of FIET reports), in the German employers' associations there is also hardly any knowledge of the collective bargaining conditions in other countries. This is, however, not perceived as a shortcoming, since, according to the opinion of the associations' representatives, Europeanisation has had hardly any influence on German collective bargaining (however, this may change in the future) or the associations and no harmonisation has been considered. There was a similar situation in Great Britain, even though the employers' associations mainly held the view that collective bargaining policy is not part of their remit.

Here, it is interesting to note, that the respective national employers' associations also represent the national interests of their countries and thus partly withhold information from their sister associations.

Currently, there is no exchange of information or even co-ordination of collective bargaining policy on the employers' side. From the point of view of the European employers'/enterprises' associations, this makes little sense anyway, since the prevailing tendency in collective bargaining policy is at the moment rather defined by catch-words such as decentralisation, flexibilisation and opening-up of collective agreements for plant agreements. In future, European co-ordination will gain importance but rather passively than actively, in order to prevent unwelcome developments such as, for example, the legal introduction of a 35-hour week in France.

The increased importance of European co-ordination for collective bargaining and the forms it takes

According to the views of both the German and the European trade unions, there will be no "big bang" of the introduction of European collective bargaining policy. Such agreements will rather develop only step-by-step and at the same time involving only certain groups of countries. The essential reason for this is the fact that the collective bargaining systems are very different in the individual European countries and the decisive factor about this is that they only form one component of the reflection of the respective 'economic and industrial orders' (Lane, 1994).[11]

For all German trade unions, a European collective bargaining policy is only in the initial stages. First, confidence between the individual trade unions should be built up. Then "soft" topics (Health and Safety, working time, etc.) should be preferred to "heavy" topics (wage, etc.). In the foreseeable future, there will be no Europeanisation which comprises all 15 countries in the same manner. Bilateral and trilateral contacts need to be built up (creating groups of countries with similar conditions according to the views of a Europe at different paces) and/or envisage regional cross-border co-operations (see treaty of Doorn, or in the area of meat and milk between Lower Saxony and the Netherlands). Basically, the national collective bargaining policy should continue to have priority by making use of the EWC and mutual agreements between the different national trade unions.

In Great Britain, the answers from the different trade unions varied very much: UNIFI, who does not see co-ordination of collective bargaining policy as an aim and the GMB expressed great scepticism and stressed that first of all it was necessary to guarantee a national co-ordination. From the point of view of GMB European targets have to be welcomed. It was, however, questionable whether the national resources of the trade unions were sufficient to put these targets into practice. The answers given by representatives of AEEU and TGWU discussed the concept of the term "Co-ordination". As long as it meant information and the development of a rough joint direction of thrust, the concept will be met with approval. Binding rules - regardless in which area - caused scepticism and rejection. Scope for autonomous national decision was insisted upon, which also included the timing of claims which are otherwise not at all controversial. Only the British construction trade union saw a basically positive prospect in increasing co-ordination.

The greatest scepticism towards a European collective bargaining policy was formulated by trade unionists from Italy and France. Most of them felt that the time for European collective agreements had not yet come. A clear priority was revealed for the national level as the decisive frame of reference for collective bargaining. None of the interviewees expected that the erosion of national collective bargaining policy could be compensated for by increased European co-ordination. The French trade unionists feared an undermining of the national standards which are traditionally, to a high

---

[11] A very good overview of the different collective bargaining systems in Europe is given in Burgess (1997, p.114).

degree, secured by the government or by law, which would be impossible to achieve within the EU.

If we try to interpret the answers of the trade unions in the four countries with a joint reference system, we have to differentiate first between five levels in the process of Europeanisation of collective bargaining policy (ordered hierarchically according to feasibility):

- information between sector of industry-specific trade unions,
- co-operation,
- co-ordination between national and European federations,
- transfer of responsibilities to the European federations,
- the melting of national (sector of industry) specific trade unions into one European trade union.

In principle, there is no co-ordination in the narrower sense of the word with a strategic objective between the trade unions in the individual countries.

Beneath the level of collective agreements there are very diverse developments in different sectors of industry: in the construction industry the concept of co-ordination seems to be wide-spread (promoted by the liberalisation of labour markets, which created a pressure to unite: also see the construction industry specific directive on postings). The general tenor is here, as well, to start first with soft topics and - also very important - to organise first of all a thorough exchange of information and knowledge about the collective bargaining conditions in the individual countries at sector of industry and enterprise level. Minimum standards and/or corridors (for working time) should be developed.

The question remains open how a - jointly co-ordinated - European collective bargaining policy should be put through (there is, for example no European right to strike). A first step would be to establish transnational solidarity, for example on specific information.

The Euro-Federations also have different views which are dominated by the characteristics of the respective sector of industry. There is an essential difference between the EFBWW (construction industry) and the EMF (metal industry) about the manner of co-ordination of collective bargaining policy: the EMF prefers a top-down approach (for example for the fixing of annual working time at 1,750 hours and an overtime quota) without knowing exactly beforehand how these limits could be put through nationally. The EFBWW favours a bottom-up approach: first it should be checked whether the national trade unions were able to put the respective agreements through. Only those fields of co-ordination would be politically tackled;

they then could be put into practice in the different countries with a relatively high probability.

The question of European collective bargaining policy is thrust upon the employers - according to their view - by the trade unions because the latter want to avoid collective bargaining dumping. A European collective bargaining policy basically did not make much sense given the tendency towards decentralisation and the move to workplace agreements. In this respect, international co-ordination is rather rejected for different reasons.

The transparency of labour costs would be the basis for a European collective bargaining policy. This will not - despite the existence of the Euro - be possible in the foreseeable future because the respective framework conditions, the work cultures and other prerequisites are very different. Furthermore a co-ordination of the European collective bargaining policy would not be desirable, at least from the point of view of "Gesamtmetall".

From the point of view of the European employers'/enterprises' associations, the European co-ordination of collective bargaining policy will of course nevertheless gain importance in the future. This importance will, however, be a negative one in so far as European co-ordination does not serve for forward design but rather for the defence of unwelcome development as, for example, the legal introduction of the 35-hour week in France. Here, the co-ordination or mutual information though is much poorer than in the trade unions.

Areas of regulation and tasks for the Europeanisation of European collective bargaining policy

For the trade unions, in principle, only "soft" topics are suitable for regulations at European level; the employers are even more reserved. There is however, no clear-cut definition of what "soft" topics are, which could thus be the subject of European collective bargaining policy. In questions of working time, collective agreements prevail in Germany, legal regulations in France. In Great Britain, this question is almost exclusively negotiated at plant level. Furthermore the national social insurance systems regulate the free movement of employees in very different ways as another field of European collective bargaining policy (Baumann, Laux and Schnepf, 1997, p. 140). Here we can find, as well, role specific differences between the protagonists which also show specific peculiarities in sectors of industry.

All German trade unionists interviewed reject European collective agreements on wage/salaries. European collective agreements for parts of the normal skeleton collective agreement (working time, holiday, employment growth, shift systems, etc.) would be thinkable and even desirable. This corresponds, by the way, to the German division of labour between skeleton collective agreements and wage agreements but also with regard to the directive on postings (i.e. limitation of the liberalisation of the labour market). Especially IG Metall continues along the path now begun of co-ordinating the claim volume and posting, that is to say that the "systematics of collective agreements" are co-ordinated.

The Italian trade unionists were much more sceptical towards European collective agreements, regardless of the concrete subject. They believed that such agreements were at least a long way ahead. In Great Britain also the trade unionists rejected this prospect on the whole - partly in accordance with the British employers - regardless of the concrete difficulties of putting them into practice.

All Euro-federations endorsed regulations on "soft" topics (qualification, working time, environmental protection, tele-work, profit sharing) as well as on topic fields which so far have not been covered by national regulations (e.g. regional cross-border co-ordination). For the foreseeable future, they excluded wage/salary as an appropriate topic for European collective agreements.

A European collective bargaining policy is anyway already hindered by the fact that there are no adequate employers' association structures at European level. The Euro-federations complain about this in particular and criticise the employers' expressed attitude of rejection towards the realisation of this aim.

On the side of the German employers' associations there is a considerable difference between "Gesamtmetall" and the employers' association in the chemical industry (the other associations do not present such a clear-cut polarisation). "Gesamtmetall" rejects European collective agreements categorically because the structural conditions are so different in the individual countries.

The employers' association in the chemical industry, however, can easily imagine collective agreements on soft topics, but not for questions of pay. In Germany alone there are 11 different wage agreements in the chemical industry. The social model "Europe" should be used as a location advantage in the triad competition. Furthermore the various lorry drivers' strikes in France, by which many companies in the west-European industry were affected, revealed that a European co-operation model is urgently needed. Here, especially the establishment of conflict settlement mechanisms is insisted on, in order to regulate the coming European Company in its core elements and to make it thus reliable.

In the construction industry there is considerable competition within the European employers' associations. The example of the posting directive makes it clear that at least in this area the similarities between trade unions and employers' associations in Germany are greater than between the employers' associations in other countries in Europe.

In Great Britain, France and Italy, the majority of employers reject the idea of moving towards European collective agreements. Only in the British construction industry was the possibility of setting-up a European framework not excluded.

Also from the point of view of the European employers'/enterprises' associations European collective agreements are a long way of: wage agreements at European level are entirely excluded and also the question of working time is not on the agenda (since this question is closely related to questions of wages). At best, negotiations on "soft" topics are conceivable from time to time, for which a special mandate would be necessary. It is interesting to note that with UNICE a trend to put European collective agreements and agreements within the Social Dialogue on the same level has begun to show.

Social Dialogue, minimum standards and role of European legislation

The above mentioned "weakness" of the European employers' associations has a direct connection to the Social Dialogue which was and is another ray of hope in the process of Europeanisation. Jacobi (1997, p. 56) assesses the (global) Social Dialogue thoroughly with categories of collective bargaining policy, and the ETUC passed a resolution in July 1999 in Helsinki which stressed the importance of the Social Dialogue for the European employment policy.

Let us make a general remark beforehand: there are basically three forms of Social Dialogue (with the first two forms belonging to the global Social Dialogue):

- Employees (ETUC), employers (UNICE) and the EU Commission jointly discuss the topic at hand and agree on a directive.
- ETUC and UNICE decide on a contract on a certain topic and thus formulate beforehand the directive for the EU Commission.
- The sectoral Social Dialogue is carried out in the form of joint statements, mostly on soft topics. Presently it is legally weak and still in its infancy. But more about this later on.

Even before the Treaty of Maastricht in 1992, ETUC, UNICE and CEEP made a joint statement on the 31.10.1991, which, in fact, was a treaty on social policy. By this, the employers wanted to weaken the EU-Commission's role of formulating and passing directives. This treaty did not, however, have the intended consequences, for example the directive on European Works Councils (directive on EWCs).

In practice the Social Dialogue often takes place as follows: first of all the EU-Commission presents the two social partners with a topic which, according to the Commission's view, should be settled by a compromise. The social partners then have nine months time to reach an agreement within the framework of the Social Dialogue. If this does not happen, the EU-Commission takes up its role as legislative body and quasi sets the standard alone, as had happened with the development of the directive on EWCs. The other directives have taken the other way - that of Social Dialogue - namely the directive on atypical employment, parental leave, part-time working and the latest framework agreement on temporary employment.

Keller (1999, p. 113) assesses the procedural results (establishment of the proceedings) of the Social Dialogue in a more positive way than the financial ones. He is sceptical towards opinions which refer to the Social Dialogue as a new quality in European industrial and social relations, if only for that reason that UNICE wants to see the existing status quo maintained at all costs. According to our view - if this results from the empirical studies presented below - the Social Dialogue is no substitute for autonomous collective bargaining, but, on the other hand, a necessary supplement to the national autonomous systems of industrial relations, thus a "European supplement" so to speak. For a further development of the Social Dialogue, mainly a strengthening of the protagonists on the European level is needed. This is, however, due to different reasons not (yet?) in sight. Furthermore, other important questions are still unanswered, for example, the one about the legal quality of these agreements; questions, which should possibly receive further clarification by a collective bargaining policy framework. Another open and also controversial question is the connection of the Social Dialogue to the European Works Councils, that is the line between the level of (legal) institutions and those of the participants: how, for example could the EWCs support the implementation of the Social Dialogue? Or even further: would it be possible that European Works Councils - also within the process of decentralization/shift towards the company level - received structuring and contractual competence within the framework of the Social Dialogue?

As far as the sectoral Social Dialogue is concerned, the new procedure, according to the social protocol, has remained almost completely without consequence, there are no framework agreements up to now (Keller, 1999,

p. 114).[12] Here, the employers are even less willing to discuss guidelines on joint topics with the trade unions and to submit them to the EU-commission for passing than they are on the level of the Social Dialogue. After all, UNICE does not make a single differentiation between sectors of industry.

As far as that goes, some national trade unionists see the way out of the weakness of the sectoral Social Dialogue mainly in co-ordinating their national collective bargaining policies (see above).

The role of the Social Dialogue, including the setting of minimum standards

In this context we asked our interview partners about:

- the tasks of the Social Dialogue, including extending it in order to fix minimum standards;
- the role of European legislation in regulating industrial relations; and
- the potential for European Works Councils to conclude collective and plant agreements at company level with the management also in order to compensate partly for the weakness of the (sectoral) Social Dialogue.

The Social Dialogue should, according to the German trade unions, fulfil two tasks (this view is shared by all trade unions irrespective of the sector of industry):

- to set minimum standards for the preparation of directives at the trans-sectoral level (preparation of concrete agreements at the sectoral level);
- to enforce the setting-up of employers' associations on a European level in order to carry out collective bargaining.

While the German and the French trade unionists take an open-minded view towards the Social Dialogue, most British trade unionists are sceptical. They criticise the few agreements that have been concluded so far as being insufficient and that it would have been better if they had not been signed. They fear that such proceedings might lead to a lowering of

---

[12] The transport business (inland navigation, sea shipping and road transport) is an exception: here European trade union federations and the employers'/enterprises' associations have reached an agreement on working time, which was submitted as a joint proposal to ETUC and UNICE with the aim of passing it as an EU-directive by the Commission.

collective bargaining standards. Additionally, they have little trust in the ability of the umbrella organisation negotiation, which, as we all know, do not carry out collective bargaining in Great Britain.

The Italian trade unions, too, are sceptical about the Social Dialogue. They fear that the envisaged minimum standards will, in fact, mark maximum standards and will thus undermine national collective bargaining policy. Again, we find the exception to the rule in the construction industry. The trade unions in charge are much more open towards European activities, from which they expect an anchoring of actual minimum standards.

In contrast to the partial scepticism at national level, all Euro-federations and the ETUC support the Social Dialogue, namely the trans-sectoral Social Dialogue as well as the sectoral one (which on the other hand, because of their function, is normally the role of the Euro-federations). It is conceivable that the negotiations on temporary employment between ETUC and UNICE (concluded in January 1999) will be supplemented by sector-specific agreements, for example on the question of temporary employment in the hotel business.

The Social Dialogue is generally regarded as the preliminary stage towards collective bargaining. According to the views of FIET, there will be very few such agreements in the future, since there are only a few areas in which sufficient similarities exist and where the pressure to agree is not so great. Another factor in the sectoral Social Dialogue is the fact that the sectors of industry are very different: employers in banking, for example, oppose the Social Dialogue vehemently and openly while the insurance business is a little less negative.

The present practice, however, also defines certain limits: on the one hand, it is a problem that the EU-Commission is withdrawing more and more from taking an active part in the regulation of industrial relations and restricts itself almost completely to the publishing of white and green papers. On the other hand, UNICE is very limited as a negotiating partner since as few as three member associations can prevent a negotiation with their veto. A malicious view is that UNICE is a 'weapon against socio-political agreements'.

The employers' associations in Germany, though, clearly have a different attitude towards the Social Dialogue and to the role of the EU-Commission. Their general opinion is: 'The Social Dialogue is a good way to prevent bad directives'. According to the German employers' associations, the EU Commission interferes in too many matters in a reglementing way, such as, for example, the EWC directive. The principle of subsidiarity is a better approach. It was conceivable to have minimum standards for the establishing of equal competitive conditions (e.g. with regard to health and safety). The Social Dialogue then makes sense if the German principle of autonomous collective bargaining holds sway, that is to say a reinforcement of the role of the social partners with the exclusion of the government.

There is a major difference between employers' associations in the metal and in the chemical industry: while Gesamtmetall thinks little of the sectoral Social Dialogue ('What are joint topics, what are they about?'), the employers' associations in the chemical industry can well image such a Dialogue, along the lines of the social partner agreements in the German chemical industry. On the whole, very few ideas emerged as to concrete contents which could bring about a solution by means of the Social Dialogue in the near future.

This at least partly open attitude towards the Social Dialogue is not shared by the British and Italian employers. Here, just as with collective bargaining policy, there is clear rejection of activities at European level.

Within the European employers' associations, there are considerable differences between individual sectors of industry. In the food industry, the Social Dialogue between UNICE and ETUC is generally welcomed; the sectoral Social Dialogue is mainly seen as an opportunity to exchange experiences and information and not as a way of negotiating agreements. The principles of subsidiarity and voluntary participation, however, have to be guaranteed.

European metal industry employers are not clear about the areas of regulation for a sectoral social Dialogue, even though WEM is making efforts to increase informal contacts with the ETUC (which is viewed critically by some member associations). The European employers in the construction industry, however, also consider the sectoral Social Dialogue to be positive. They are increasingly moving away from confrontation. The Social Dialogue should, however, generally remain concentrated on "soft" or company-related topics. Even in the construction industry, though, binding agreements should at least not always be seen as main objectives, in many cases a mutual exchange of information is good enough on its own.

The role of European legislation in shaping industrial relations

Here, the German trade unions were clearly split. IG BCE and HBV want to abandon the old idea of 'Seize political power and then the legislature will do the rest' and increasingly want to support dialogue and persuasive debate, at the end of which the legislature only sanctions what the social partners have already agreed. IG Metall, NGG and IG BAU, on the other hand, emphasise the responsibility of the European legislature in this area

('If we take European unification seriously'). At the same time though, they demand a considerably more important role for the European Parliament.

Even in the UK and France the trade unions expected that a stronger role for the legislature in setting minimum standards would be an advantage and that is why they supported such activities. However, they argued at the same time to retain the national action in order to be able to take better account of each national situation.

The basic approach of the European trade union federations is to maintain the present practice: a strict compliance with the principle of subsidiarity. Only where there is no voluntary agreement between the social partners should the legislature - or the Commission - intervene. This is to put pressure on the employers to negotiate in a result-orientated way (for example in areas such as reduction of weekly working time, health and safety, taxation, new forms of work organisation, atypical employment, problems of transnational social insurance law, etc).

At the same time, the Commission/ the European legislature was criticised and the following requirements were formulated:

- a legal deregulation has taken place over the last few years, which should now be "ironed out".
- recently, minimum standards have been introduced only very sluggishly by the legislative; the Commission has not launched any relevant bills over the last two years;
- there are major difficulties with the introduction of minimum standards which should be more than just setting standards at the lowest level; and
- There should be a constitutional basis for the action of the collective bargaining parties in Europe, e.g. non-discrimination, equal opportunities, basic labour and social rights (minimum wage?) and the right to strike. The right to strike should, however, not be overestimated, since it is already possible today to co-ordinate sufficient trade union industrial action in order to reach the envisaged aims.

German employers' associations are united in their rejection of the EU Commission as legislative body. The Commission is accused of violating the principle of subsidiarity, as, for example in the directive on EWCs. In Germany, alone, there is a labyrinth of regulations which they do not want to see extended to the European level. The draft paper for a directive on consultation and information at company level was given as another negative example. This draft paper could not be put into practice in

Germany, since it contained concepts which do not exist at all in German law. The legislature should only interfere in a regulatory way in German socio-political matters if at all; if the Social Dialogue has been exhausted and if autonomous collective bargaining is maintained; if the principles of subsidiarity and favourableness giving priority to individual plant level regulations over generalising regulations are observed. In this case, the European Parliament, and not the Commission should deal with the legislation.

It is interesting that employers show a general acceptance of minimum standards by the EU-Commission. They stressed, however, that legal European regulations there should be alone and that the national differences and peculiarities have to be maintained.

The European employers' associations attach great importance to the consideration of subsidiarity: the European legislature should only become involved if the national parliaments declare that it is not their responsibility (a precondition for this would be a transfer of responsibility which the employers do not want). The present flexibility should be retained and, if possible, extended. In all European countries there is a current trend towards deregulation in the sense of a shift to regulation, e.g. to the company level. Europe should not back this trend. There are anyway only a few areas where European regulations are significant (this is especially true for Health and Safety protection). The more the regulations tend to deal with "heavier" topics, the lower is the acceptance of European measures.

"Europeanisation" of collective bargaining policy within a multi-level framework of regulation

The "Europeanisation" of collective bargaining policy apparently takes place as a multi-layered process where the national level remains of great importance. One reason for this lies in the refusal of employers to negotiate seriously on the European level or to build up respective negotiating structures in the first place. On the other hand, there is also wide-spread scepticism towards European negotiations among the trade unions. This is due to the question of how far the trade unions believe that they have their matters dealt with outside the national framework.

Consequently, the legislature has considerable importance for national collective agreements in a broader sense on the European level, which, however, can only be carried out to a small degree. A second field of collective agreements emerges at the enterprise level, where the EWCs would have to take on an important role. Whether the EWCs can fulfil this task or whether they should take this task on from the trade unions' point of view, cannot be clearly answered at the moment.

The co-ordination of national collective bargaining policies at European level seems to be the main form of Europeanisation at the moment. National organisations and agreements will continue to predominate for the foreseeable future. From this perspective, the dispute about a "productivity orientated collective bargaining policy vs. national employment pacts" is, however, put into context. Instead, it will be decisive as to what extent the national employment pacts are compatible with European co-ordination or which elements have to be pushed back due to the requirements of European solidarity (also see on this topic: Marginson and Sisson, 1998; Goldbach and Schulten, 1999; Traxler, 1996).

On the employers' side developments seem to be following the formation of collective bargaining policy inside the national frameworks. Employers do not have an interest in a uniform European collective bargaining policy, not even in a European-wide co-ordination. This will only develop, if the trade unions are strong enough to put this topic on the agenda.

5. Relations between national and European levels of industrial relations - five case studies

The general considerations above should now be put into concrete form through case studies which deal with the links between the national and European level of industrial relations within the process of corporate restructuring.

By doing so, we want to illustrate that in practice, there are different connections between national and European levels of labour relations. The possibility of acting solely at national or solely at European level does not offer a potential solution to the problem.

Altogether, within the framework of the project, we conducted five case studies which are now outlined in the following overview:

Case study 1:
Merger of Alusuisse Lonza Group AG with VIAG.
Conglomerate, predominantly metal and chemical industry; sites in Germany, Great Britain, and Switzerland were examined.

Case study 2:
Restructuring measures at Electrolux-Zanussi.
Metal industry company; sites in Italy, France, and Germany were examined.

Case study 3:
Restructuring measures at company ABC.[13]
Production company; sites in France, Italy, and Germany.

---

[13] This company remains anonymous throughout this report.

Case study 4:
Restructuring measures of Kaefer-Isoliertechnik (Insulating technology).
Building company; two sites in Germany.

Case study 5:
Restructuring measures at Zeneca.
Chemical and pharmaceutical company; plants in Great Britain and Germany were examined.

These examples were chosen as case studies because:

- Different kinds of restructuring measures were implemented; e.g. external merger and internal (job cuts, cost reduction) etc.;
- company headquarters are based in different countries;
- several countries are affected;
- in all companies there is an EWC, each with different national representation;
- the bodies representing worker interests display different attitudes and ways of working.

These aspects allow for a comparison that promises deep insights into the different ways of functioning in the relations between national and European levels of representation.

In the order and comparison of the cases we proceed on a three-sided relational system of the EWC. According to this, the EWC is poised at the point where the expectancy of the three different groups coincides - national workplace representatives, management and trade unions.[14] The very tense relationship is further complicated by the fact that it is possible to distinguish between company headquarters and national locations on the side of the management and between European federations and national associations on the side of the trade unions. The structures of union federations vary from country to country. Furthermore, it is possible to distinguish between national representation bodies (organised quite differently, even on the national level) and national workforces whose demands and expectations need not automatically be identical.

We do not want to followup the multitude of these distinctions here. But, it is quite obvious that the EWC finds itself in a complex position and situation. The EWC's influence as an institution tends to be restricted by its lack of power. It is only able to develop an efficient (political)

---

[14] cf. the interesting deliberations of Fürstenberg on the German works council in Fürstenberg (1958).

practice if it is accepted by those involved, in combination with the opportunity to get enough information and at the same time, if it is has a concept of its own activities. This applies especially to the development of its own view of how it should operate as an EWC, the mastering of communication and information problems both within the EWC and externally, as well as the development of a strategy to guide its day-to-day activities.

The complex correlations are explained in the figure below and these will be applied to all the cases studied.

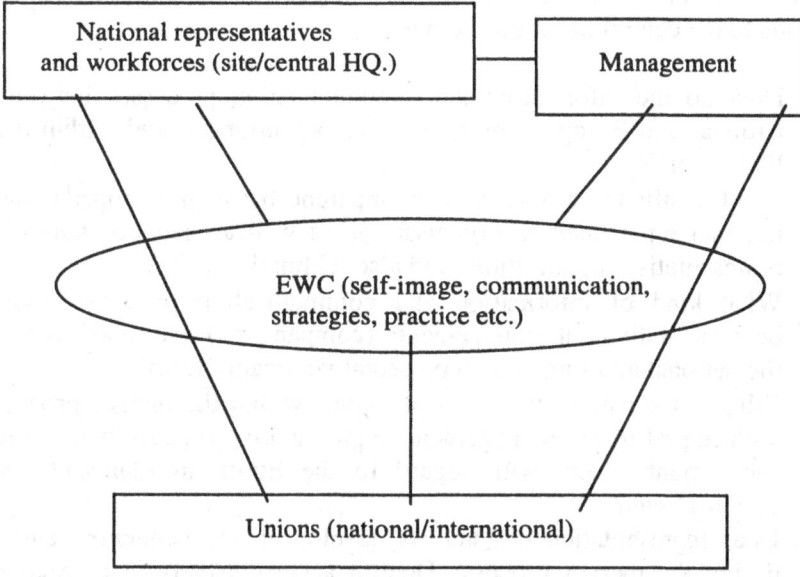

Figure 5.1   The EWC and its interaction partners

For the purposes of presenting the case studies we are using the same order. After the description of the concept and target of the individual case study, a detailed description of the companies and the restructuring they are involved will follow. This will be supplemented by a general analysis of the EWC, and a description of its situation and function within the restructuring process.

Case Study 1: The European Works Council of Alusuisse Lonza (algroup) within the planned merger of the algroup with VIAG

Concept and goal of the case study

The main topic of this case study is the eventually unsuccessful merger of Alusuisse Lonza and VIAG. The focus is on Alusuisse Lonza and only a marginal reference to VIAG. The case study analyses the situation and function of the European Works Council (EWC) and the representative organisations from each country during the merger process.

The basic issue is how industrial relations institutions and processes interact and correlate at European and national level.
This leads to the central questions below:

- How do the information and communication processes between national and European representative organisations and within the EWC work?
- What conflicts of interest are apparent between European and national representative organisations as well as between national representative organisations and also within the EWC?
- What kind of information and communication processes exist between individual managements (company and subsidiaries) and the national and European representative organisations?
- What is the role of the national unions within the merger process with regard to the management, representative organisations from each country, and with regard to the European representative organisations?
- Does representation of interests develop an independent position during the merger process? Does it act exclusively in a reactive way or does it pursue individual goals on the offensive?
- What are the expectations of the management with regard to representation of interests; what is the role of representation of interests within the management's strategic and tactical considerations?
- How does the national workforce rank questions on representation of interests on the European level and what is their interest?

These questions were taken up with the help of a combination of several methods of analysis and empirical tools:

- analysis of documents and contents of a range of company material (business reports, news releases, EWC contracts etc.), press reports, minutes of EWC conferences;
- participation in and observation of EWC meetings about the planned merger, including pre-meetings and follow-up meetings;
- discussions between the experts and the EWC chairman and vice chairman (Germany and Great Britain), the trade union experts of the EWC (Switzerland, Germany, and Great Britain), representatives of the human resources management from the company headquarters (Switzerland) as well as national management representatives (Germany and Great Britain).

Alusuisse Lonza Group AG and the merger with VIAG

Alusuisse Lonza Group AG - an overview Algroup is a diversified international conglomerate with headquarters in Zürich, Switzerland. The company was founded in Neuhaus, Switzerland in 1888. It was Europe's first aluminium foundry; in 1974, the company expanded through the acquisition of the Swiss chemicals company Lonza and renamed Alusuisse Lonza. After the acquisition of the Canadian packing company Lawson Mardon Group (1994) and the packing company Wheaton (1996) further strategic acquisitions followed.

The conglomerate has an international/global orientation and is diversified into five core segments. Since the beginning of the nineties, the company has pursued a target-oriented portfolio management strategy where the business portfolio is aimed at segments with a higher value potential. This policy would have culminated in the planned merger with VIAG in 1999 as a "merger of equals".

The conglomerate is organised in five divisions (figures from 1997):

- Alusuisse Aluminium Production (turnover of 1.7 billion, CHF, 1,693 employees).
  and Alusuisse Aluminium Processing (turnover of 2.0 billion CHF, 7,337 employees).
- Lawson Mardon Food and Tobacco Packaging (turnover of 1.8 billion CHF, 6,384 employees).
- Wheaton Pharmaceutical and Cosmetic Packaging (turnover of 1.2 billion CHF, workforce of 7,569 employees).
- Lonza Fine and Speciality Chemicals (turnover of 1.4 billion CHF, 4.313 employees).
- Lonza Intermediate Products and Additives (turnover of 0.6 billion CHF, 1,032 employees).

The total proceeds of the company according to the 1998 business report:

Net Turnover   8,581 million CHF (+5.4% in comparison with previous year);
Net Profit   530 million CHF (+ 14.5% in comparison with previous year);
Workforce   29,495 (- 5.1% in comparison with previous year).

The company has production locations and sales markets throughout the world with a focus on the EU, North America, and Switzerland, but also other European countries, South America, Asia and Australia.

The European Works Council agreement covers 10 countries in total with approximately 20,000 employees, that is around two-thirds of the company's total workforce. Switzerland, Germany, and Great Britain have the highest number of participants. It is noticeable that Germany and especially Great Britain have experienced a massive reduction in workplaces in recent years, while in other countries only a few workplaces have been shut down or their number has remained stable.

The key element of the Algroup company culture is the objective of being 'best-in-its class' as advocated by company chair, S. Marchionne. This is often quoted by the EWC - occasionally in a critical and ironic way.

The company's culture can be characterised by the following statements:

- Vision of Algroup: 'We want to be the leading, most diversified industrial group that is 'best in class' - in every business sector...'.
- Culture of Algroup: 'Less bureaucracy, fewer regulations; investing first in human resources, then in other resources...'.
- Leading competencies of Algroup: 'Result-orientated; personal pursuit of knowledge, courage to lead others; etc.'.

These guiding and management principles are issued to every manager in short form on a card resembling a credit card when joining the company (Financial Times, Feb. 15th, 1999).

There is a company-wide Human Resource Management department - albeit covering only management positions. The group's language is English. All of the leading managers have had work experience abroad.

Merger of Alusuisse Lonza and VIAG - key features of the deal   The 1999 merger was supposed to create a group with a well-balanced portfolio based on two mainstays: energy and telecommunication activities as well as industrial/manufacturing activities (Packaging, Aluminium, Speciality

Chemicals). With a workforce of 127,000, the new group would be the sixth biggest industrial company in Germany, the biggest in Switzerland, and no. 26 in Europe. Headquarters would be located in Munich.

The management of both companies see the merger as complementary and forecast extraordinary synergy in their industrial activities. It was expected that the most notable efficiency improvements would result from the amalgamation of production, purchase, distribution and marketing (especially for aluminium and packaging) as well as reduced fixed costs at group and sector level. The workforce would be reduced by approximately 2% of the current total of 127,000, i.e. 2,500 jobs will go. The reduction in employment was supposed to be achieved through early retirement (where possible) and natural wastage. According to the group management, job cuts would only affect management positions.

Although the merger is expressly seen by the managements as a "merger of equals", Algroup was significantly the minor partner. A few facts about the structure of VIAG make this clear:

VIAG is active in five core areas: energy, telecommunications, packaging, aluminium and chemicals. The company employs approx. 95,000 people. From Algroup's point of view, energy (Bayernwerk) and telecommunications (VIAG Interkom) are new sectors, while other areas are more or less identical to Algroup divisions. The management assumes these sectors would complement each other.

The merger should have been completed by August 1999. From the beginning, there were doubts about achieving a trouble-free and successful merger. According to the Financial Times (February 15th, 1999), Alusuisse shareholders were concerned about the fact that the new group would be active in two business sectors where some uncertainties are involved: nuclear energy (Bayernwerk) especially when considering the announced draw-back from nuclear energy in Germany, and the very risky telecommunications sector.

Moreover the stock exchange, according to the Financial Times, is increasingly unhappy about large mergers of diversified conglomerates. In addition, criticism was levelled at the group's chairman Sergio Marchionne. How can a man who does not even speak German and who is seen as a representative of the shareholder value approach to business, be successful in coping with the task of leading (as co-leader) a more or less German company that is subject to the co-determination of the workforce (Financial Times, February 13th/14th 1999)?

Finally it was remarked that possibly in Switzerland - and so too the different shareholders (probably with the exception of some major shareholders) as well as for the worker's representative bodies - the merger of a traditional Swiss company with a significantly larger German group could be regarded, partly explicitly partly subliminally, as not necessarily being a "merger of equals" as promised, but a kind of sell-out.

On March 29th, 1999, an algroup press release announced that the merger negotiations with VIAG had been terminated. The reason stated was the demand to change the originally agreed share quota from 65% (VIAG) and 35% (Algroup) to 67,5% and 32,5%, following the conclusions of an expert opinion. Both companies expressed their disappointment about the failure of the merger which - only a short time before - VIAG chairman, W. Simson, had described as a 'quantum leap' in terms of the company's evolution. At the same time, it was clearly expressed that the struggle over the share quota was only a pretext. Simson was confronted in an interview with the assumption of people who knew the sector industry that he was only trying to prevent the occupation of important key positions of the new combine by Swiss managers (Der Spiegel, 14/1999, p. 79).

We do not want to speculate further on the reasons behind the failed merger, but it is our opinion that it could have something to do with - if not primarily - the focus of our studies, industrial relations; but more on this later.

The facts are that both companies announced their intention to go ahead with the development of their individual strategic goals. Meanwhile, VIAG has announced its merger with the German group VEBA. Algroup is pursuing a triple merger with the Canadian Alcan combine and the French Pechiney group 'in order to create the largest aluminium conglomerate worldwide and the worldwide leading company within the business sector of flexible and special packaging', according to the wording of an Algroup press release. This merger is not a focus of the underlying case study and will not be followed-up in this document.

What we do want to do is to analyse the industrial relations problems in this specific case, i.e. the role and function of the EWC within the process of the planned merger against the background of the described data and developments.

The structures and processes of the EWC

Founding and Structure of the EWC In the spring of 1996, the group's management proposed setting up an EWC taking as models agreements in the Swiss chemicals industry, i.e. weak on rights and in accordance with the French forum model. This proposal was met with resistance by the EMF (European Metal Workers' Federation) among others.

Later on, a day seminar was organised at the Alusuisse Singen site where there were traditionally co-operative industrial relations between the company director, the plant level representation and the IG Metall (Metal workers' union). The foundation stone of the EWC was laid at this seminar. There was still resistance from the Swiss management who complained about the failure to take account of Swiss non-industrial employees in the EWC.[15] This was criticised by the French, who thought themselves underrepresented on the EWC. Finally, these (and other problems) were solved so that on September 18th 1996 the agreement was finally signed setting up a European Works Council and covering the arrangements for informing and consulting employees of European companies of the Alusuisse-Lonza Group.

The agreement was expressly finalised as defined by art. 13 of the EWC directive. It is strange that Alusuisse-Lonza Europe BV acts as the representative of the company, a company registered according to Dutch law with headquarters in Breda. It would have been more fitting to establish the central management in Zürich or Singen. Management possibly actively prevented the latter in order not to have the EWC set up within the environment of the far-reaching German system of co-determination. Employees regarded this decision 'as a bitter pill which one had to swallow'. On the other hand, the agreement has positive aspects that exceed the minimum standard of the EWC directive. This applies less to the information rights of the EWC, which show no special modifications - neither positive nor negative - from the directive and its subsidiary provisions. Nevertheless, their successes included getting three union experts for the EWC, who have to be financed by the central management.

The EWC has 16 representatives from 10 countries according to the company size. Switzerland, Great Britain, and Germany - as locations with a minimum of 20% of the total of employees have three representatives each; Austria, France, Iceland, Ireland, Italy, The Netherlands, and Spain have one representative each. Only one woman is among the representatives.

The EWC represents approx. 20,000 employees in the above countries. Non-European countries are not covered. It is significant that every country in Europe has a representative, e.g. even Austria, with only 74 employees at the time. Similar to other EWC agreements, it is in no way self-evident that the EWC represents minority positions such as Austria's.

The chairman of the EWC is from Germany. This is mainly for organisational reasons, since he is, at the same time, the full-time chairman of the German works council and therefore has (supposedly) more working flexibility than his Swiss and British colleagues. As he is simultaneously

---

[15] There is a dual system of representation of interests within companies in Switzerland: Operational committees elected by all employees and separate committees for white-collar workers.

engaged in several other honorary functions for the union, it is clear that he has a lot of work to do. His deputy is a shop steward from a British company and father of the chapel (honorary chairperson) of the local GPMU (Graphical Paper and Media Union). Together with a worker representative from the company from Switzerland they form the presidium of the EWC - the so-called special committee of the EWC that can meet in between the EWC conferences, instead of calling an extraordinary EWC meeting.

The EWC has three full-time trade union experts (IG Metall, Germany; SMUV (Union Industry, Trade, Services), Switzerland; and GPMU (Graphical, Paper and Media Union), Great Britain, who have an unrestricted right to attend and participate in all conferences.

The EWC meets annually in a regular conference; extraordinary EWC conferences in special circumstances are, of course, always possible.

General problems and development of the EWC

Regarding the working principles of the EWC (information, organisation, co-operation) The EWC has existed for three years now. With one regular conference per year, complemented by two extraordinary conferences and meetings of the special committee, coping with the work is without question quite a small job. If we compare it with the experiences of worker representatives from specific countries, as in the case of the German works council or the British shop steward, then it is clear that the practices which have developed, reliable proceedings, and development of the new fields of problems and topics can only be created by a long-term learning process - a process that is far from finished. This is a difficult problem many of the recently formed EWCs are facing - the Algroup EWC is no exception.

At an EWC conference pre-meeting in 1998, there was considerable criticism within the EWC of previous working methods; this applied especially to the special committee's and the president's (chairperson) information policy. Several representatives complained about the fact that they had received no information at all or that they were provided with information far too late to be of any use. It became obvious then

> that one of the main failures of the European Works Council (is) that it is not possible or even that it should not be allowed to do it as a side job (quoted from the meeting's minutes).

Some representatives demanded that the main job of the chairperson should be the work within the EWC - a proposition that was and is rarely practicable for the chairperson taking account of his tasks in his national company.[16] As a result, there were demands for the company management to provide the EWC chairperson with the necessary staffing for the required secretarial work that comes with this task. In the meantime, the company management have agreed to and provided two secretaries with language skills as staff support for the chairperson. In addition an improvement in the working conditions of the special committee was agreed to, so that it will now be able to meet four times a year.

This allows for improvements to the co-ordination of and preparation for EWC meetings. But, in the opinion of everybody concerned, there is still an urgent need to develop a clear structure and to set out the defined goals of the EWC. This applies especially to the working arrangements between EWC conferences. Although communication between individual EWC members has been improving in recent months, it is not yet sufficiently systemised and sometimes relies on pure coincidence.

> We have to make clear that EWC work continues throughout the year, it is not limited to the annual conference (from an interview with the deputy EWC chairperson).

The co-operation with national unions is one of the positive results of the EWC's work, especially with those that send their union experts; co-operation with the EMF as one of the responsible Euro-federations is also considered to be very good. Despite this good news, a general structural problem exists. The deputy EWC chairperson as well as the British union expert are members of the GPMU. The German counterpart is in IG Medien and not IG Metall, and, in Brussels, not the EMF. In our case study, as we have seen, co-operation is achieved without any problems. But other arrangements are possible, where different national union structures could lead to serious tensions.

The connection to national representatives is ambivalent according to our findings. On the one hand, the connection is working because of the personal union of the EWC members as national representatives. On the other hand other national representatives, who are not members of the EWC, demonstrate rather low commitment to and interest in the EWC. For them, restructuring affecting plants in their own country is far more important than the EWC topic (Germany). Or the EWC seems completely alien to them, and the information they are given does not affect their situation much (Great Britain). There is even less interest in the EWC among "simple" union members and the workforce.

---

[16] The chairperson is busy with massive re-structuring measures of the company she/he is employed with. His EWC activity can not be a "main" job - it has always to be an additional task.

Another difficulty is displayed by the EWC as an international body for the practical way of working. Finding consent solutions is a lot more complicated than on the national level, and asks for "diplomatic" skills. This makes the whole thing tough and slow (interview EWC-chairperson). This leads to problems which are probably common to all EWCs.

Language and cultural problems for the EWC

Language problems were obvious at the EWC meeting we observed The whole meeting, including pre-meetings and follow-up sessions, was simultaneously translated. There is no common language for all delegates. Communication outside the meeting therefore only happened in selected ways. Two of the German delegates spoke English and used this for some very detailed discussions with their British colleagues. Two of the three Swiss delegates also spoke German, so they communicated without difficulty with the Germans and Austrians. The British seemed to speak only English, the French only French, etc. The EWC chairman confirmed, that communication

> without an interpreter was very difficult. English helps a little in private, but not when discussing the issues (interview with EWC chairman).

The reasons for this are well-known and shall not be discussed any further. This was in marked contrast to the management representatives present, who could all communicate in English without difficulty. In fact, by the way, they pointed out that: In management there are no comparable cultural differences. Whoever wants to succeed here has to be able to deal with various cultures. The managers of Algroup all have international experience (interviews with group management).

Whether or not one considers this right or wrong,[17] there is a dramatic difference in competence between management and the EWC, which makes the EWC's work even harder.

The question of national differences is not just about language, as we noted as observers in the meeting.

At various points it became clear that there are different local interests (at least subliminal conflicts of interests between the Swiss and Germans, as was assumed by some of the Swiss) as well as different mentalities (e.g. Italian and Spanish representatives demanding action, though not in a very precise way) as well as different ways of working (the British beginning by

---

[17] Lane (1989) and Eberwein and Tholen (1993) showed that there are, partly significant, cultural differences between managers of different nationalities.

making the conflict an issue concerning the question of the information policy, accentuating co-operation by the Germans and the Swiss).

The conflicts and problems raised here lead directly to the question of training of EWC members.

The EWC and training

The EWC repeatedly asked management to provide training and this was not rejected out of hand. Yet, so far the EWC has not set out an agreed formula for training which could have been put to a management which seems fully prepared to make concessions. In the meantime the following has been agreed with management:

- individual training for EWC-members, especially language courses and use of modern communication systems; these are to be paid for by the central office, contrary to the former regulations.
- training for the EWC as a body; the EWC is to prepare a training programme for this (interviews with EWC-chairman and German trade union expert).

Only time will tell the extent to which all this will be carried out. In any case it is up to the EWC itself to take advantage of the possibilities offered by management.

The management's assessment of the EWC

Apart from the fact, that the management constantly argues about the costs involved (especially for simultaneous interpretations), the managers we interviewed all spoke positively about the EWC, yet with certain subtle distinctions depending on the national viewpoint.

Representatives of central management stressed that, from their point of view, they were happy with the EWC. They rejected any changes to the rules in the light of the forthcoming review of the EWC Directive. Above all they do not want a system of co-determination. This is also the case for employees, 'as long as conditions are not equal'. Cultural differences were repeatedly mentioned as the biggest problem for the EWC (interviews with central management).

From the German point of view, the EWC has no great importance for either the company or the management,

> as we have the most developed system of co-determination. We are only extending to a European level a part of what we do in every-day-life

anyway. It is different though for other countries and for some German enterprises which do not work with unions. In such cases, the EWC is necessary, or better useful (interviews with German management).

According to the British management view, the EWC is still in the "embryonic phase". The biggest problem is language. It is also not very clear, which subjects are to be dealt with by the EWC (interview with British management).

All in all, management representatives seem to accept the EWC. This is no doubt because of the merger process, in which the management needs the support of the EWC - this will be examined in more detail later.

First, though, we consider how those actually involved assess the EWC.

The EWC and its development as judged by its main participants

Most of the participants interviewed made a critical and very sober assessment of the EWC, although almost all of them showed cautious optimism about its development and future potential. The chairman said:

> The EWC started off very tentatively. There were mainly communication problems. But then, the conferences got better, and, in particular, co-operation improved. The main success has been the constant improvement in management's information policy, which although not very good is adequate for the time being. Up to now, there has only been language training for a minority
>
> Otherwise, the EWC has not been able to achieve that much, maybe a few changes in the heads leading the company. It has not succeeded in developing the scope of its activities like the German works council has.
> In the long term, a European wage policy should be agreed upon - this will only be possible with an EWC that works. In the medium term, the EWC should be the means to establishing a European health and safety and environmental policy.
>
> With regard to internal company problems such as wages, working conditions, working time and such it is no longer possible to play the national representatives off against one another, as now we can just ask the British, for example (interview with the EWC chairman).

The trade union experts and most of the delegates of the EWC share the opinion that: 'The EWC is developing step by step' (interviews with union experts from Switzerland and Germany, minutes of participating observers). The merger discussion was the key influence on management's policy on providing information to the EWC - although this does not mean that the EWC is consulted in all strategic matters, or is, in fact, integrated into the decision-making process. Furthermore, it was noted that the EWC has helped strengthen the "underdeveloped" Swiss representative structures.

Although he comes from a completely different area of industrial relations, similar conclusions are reached by the deputy chairperson of the EWC:

> Although considerable progress has been made, this has been limited to the EWC itself and has not had an impact on employees. This is the reason why the workforce does not really appreciate the EWC very much. One can only guess what is going on in companies without EWCs. The EWC ensures a certain transparency regarding actual conditions. In short: we have become independent of management propaganda.

Currently, the EWC's influence on industrial relations in Great Britain is very limited, simply because few EWC have been set up.

> During the next five-year period, the work of the EWC will change dramatically: The EWC will find itself increasingly integrated into negotiations at European level. A key issue of debate in the light of the merger has been whether a joint redundancy policy for all Algroup companies should be developed. The EWC can also work to the advantage of company management: as a result of many mergers, multinational corporations can no longer be controlled. The new merger would create a workforce of 95,000. "Intermediaries" are needed. To a certain extent, it can be argued that establishing an EWC is just the first step on the road to a larger institution, for example a World Works Council.
>
> If Britain adopted the Euro as its currency there would be greater transparency on pay and the EWC would play a more important role in collective bargaining. And there is no alternative, because if a joint approach is not adopted, the result will be low wages and jobs will be under threat (interview with the deputy EWC chairman).

Similar statements were expressed in interviews by full-time trade union officials from Britain: Currently, the EWC is still relatively unknown in the UK and British EWC members were not in a position to challenge management. In the future though, the EWCs could become very important and complement other trade union structures in order to extend collective bargaining to the European level.

These "visions" set out the possibilities for future development and interaction at European and national level.

In reality, of course, a different picture emerges as the current tasks and problems facing the algroup EWC demonstrate. Apart from the problems of improving the EWC's working arrangements and its training provision which have already been mentioned, there is also the admission of the CEE states (Czech Republic, Slovenia, Hungary) to be added to the agenda.

Above all, the EWC is constantly busy dealing with issues arising from the company's future strategy. We now want to outline the EWC's limitations by looking at its place and role in the merger process with VIAG.

Position and role of the EWC within the merger process

Information from Algroup management The EWC chairman and the deputy chairman only became aware of the planned merger informally, having been notified by a journalist. An extraordinary EWC conference was scheduled in December 1998. This conference was called off by the group management due to "organisational reasons" and replaced by a meeting of the special committee. During this meeting the EWC complained about getting such inadequate information about the merger. The EWC was informed by fax just 30 minutes (!) before the press conference where the merger plans were publicly disclosed. The Financial Times had actually reported on the merger before the EWC was officially notified.

At the extraordinary EWC conference that we observed, the Algroup head explained what had happened:

> This course of events was not planned by us at all. The "merger project" was initiated in 1998 by a small group of people. At the time, someone from the company had unfortunately been indiscrete about the merger when talking to a Financial Times journalist in New York, who immediately published his information. We do not know who committed the indiscretion. We will improve our information policy and I apologise for these unfortunate developments (notes from participating observers).

Furthermore, even the management representatives at national level interviewed by us stated that they only became aware of the merger plans by reading the newspaper. The same applies to group managers who were interviewed.

At the extraordinary EWC conference it became obvious that top management was trying to establish a more open information policy towards the EWC. This was evidence by the presence of the CEO and was in fact emphasised by him directly.[18] The possible intention was to integrate the EWC into the merger process in order to avoid any resistance

---

[18] Within the planned merger, the information policy of the management with regard to the EWC was definitely improving (interview with the deputy EWC chairman).

to the merger. Moreover, the CEO's information policy was generally the target of criticism in the media and this 'is sometimes much more effective than all of our demands' (interview with a trade union expert).

The hitherto inadequate information policy is one of the core topics of the extraordinary EWC conference on the merger.

The extraordinary EWC conference on the merger

The conference was opened by the EWC chairman and began with a report on the merger from the CEO. Key details on this have already been mentioned. The central message was that:

> The workforce is our prime concern - not the shareholders. The unions do not fully understand the merger. It is our goal to become the best servicing company in the world. This is a unique merger: It is not a question of rationalisation simply to cut the number of employees. We need competent and committed workers.

This statement is contradicted by, for example, articles in the Financial Times from February 15th, 1999 that show the CEO focussing more on shareholder value. Otherwise, the CEO's report was quite open. However, most of the information disclosed was already available via Internet. At the same time, it seemed remarkable to us that the CEO himself was presenting the facts to the EWC. This was certainly a symbolic act with strategic intentions behind it.

Subsequently, questions from the EWC were put by the chairman with the help of a list of queries put together during a pre-meeting of delegates.

The CEO answered the questions willingly and more or less openly. He obviously made an effort to demonstrate there and then the promised improvement in the company's approach to providing information. This was maybe the reason too, why he made a personal appearance. It was significant that he answered all of the questions himself.

The EWC conference ended at noon although it was scheduled to end in the early evening. The main reason for this was the lack of further questions or comments and independent opinions from the EWC either about the merger or on the question of training.

The management adopted a very co-operative manner - which had not always been the case in the past. To a certain extent, there would have perhaps been some opportunity to win additional concessions if any demands had been put forward. In our opinion the key reason for this openness has already been mentioned: the management wanted to cover its back in case that workforce and their representatives were planning to interfere with the merger. This is probably connected with the general public criticism of the management's inadequate information policy. On the other hand it could also be management's reaction to confronting the German co-determination structure in VIAG. This argument appeared later in press reports and could be overheard during the meeting as well.

The improved information policy was the most notable success of the EWC conference. Most delegates had a positive view of the conference and its outcome. At the same time, it was obvious that there was a need to question management more closely during the conference in order to take full advantage of the group's offer of more information.

The role of the EWC during the merger

In our opinion the management wanted the EWC to help facilitate the merger without developing its own views on the process. Management saw it as acting as a mediator between management and national representatives, trade unions and the workforce.

No conflicts between the national representatives, the EWC and unions were experienced, although nearly all the various national representatives had a different focus of interest.

This was not due to the fact that the EWC deliberately accepted the position of mediator, but more a result of the fact that neither the EWC nor the unions nor the representatives themselves had or could have had a clear conception of the possible effects of the merger. The EWC had certainly put together information from different sides but it is still difficult to develop a view when you are mainly acting upon rumours. Overall, the EWC played a more active role than before, but it was still only re-acting to the actions of others (interview with a trade union expert). The EWC chairman in a critical self-assessment said:

> The EWC, in particular the special committee, should have reacted earlier. Our information policy was good. We just assumed that the merger had already gone through. Otherwise we would have increased the pressure on management (interview with EWC chairman).

The failure of the merger

In retrospect, the merger - if it had worked - was seen as a positive step by most of those interviewed. This was because there was a good chance that several sites could have been given a guarantee by management about their future. After the merger collapsed some plants could only fear the worst.

There was a high degree of consensus that the question of the companies' valuation was definitely not the only reason the merger failed.

During the merger process, it was always obvious that there was a major difference between VIAG's German stakeholder-orientated corporate culture based on co-determination and Algroup's Anglo-American, shareholder-oriented approach as personified by the CEO. With this in mind, the reservations about the chief executive published in "Der Spiegel" and the "Financial Times" (see above) seem not totally unfounded. If this is correct, the failed merger is a good example of the role that different systems of industrial relations can play within these kinds of processes and of the effects of their interaction.

Conclusion: The EWC between acceptance and functionalising

In our opinion, generalising from the detailed example of the EWC Algroup, the case can be characterised as an example of an "EWC between acceptance and functionalising". In adopting this description, we are applying the concept of the EWC in a complex net of relations (see above). This puts the EWC in a web of relationships with national organisations representing employees, the workforce itself, the management, and the unions. The EWC has to move within this complex power structure, with only limited authority. The EWC can only work in practice, if it can be sure of being accepted by the others, if it is able to set up an exchange of information and at the same time come up with a concept of what it is supposed to be doing. This includes developing a clear view of itself as an EWC, tackling the problems relating to communication and information both within and outside the EWC, as well as developing a suitable strategy to guide its activities.

Let us relate the general context to the concrete case. We demonstrated that the EWC went through a development and learning process in the first few years of its existence. This process led to a clear, if still incomplete, improvement in its ways of working and communicating. At the same time the EWC developed a clearly defined image of itself in terms of its relationship with central management. The EWC as a committee clearly adopts a co-operative approach, that is written into the agreement, but which is not at all obvious to all the EWC members when considering their own national systems of industrial relations. There is an open atmosphere within the EWC and it clearly strives to reach a consensus. Overall, the EWC sees itself - according to our findings - as a unified committee that can openly express the expectations and demands of the workforce that it represents. At the same time, this does mean that there is not an open discussion about differing local interests.

There is agreement that the EWC is not a body that provides representation in the sense of co-determination.

Overall it can be said that the EWC has a clear perception of its own activities. Despite certain improvements in the merger process, it is still a point of criticism that the EWC has not developed its own strategy that would allow it to be less re-active in the future.

On the whole the relationship between the EWC and the unions appears to be one of mutual acceptance. The EWC is critically dependant upon the support it gets from unions, especially from the three union experts. This is not necessarily self-evident if the British example above is considered, where for a long time the unions had a quite sceptical attitude to the EWC. Moreover, there do not appear to be any conflicts between the national unions with regard to the EWC.

The relations of the EWC to the national bodies representing employees and to the employees themselves are ambivalent. We were able to make it clear that acceptance of the EWC arose mainly from the fact that the national employee representatives were also themselves EWC members. This was the reason for the fact that there were almost no conflicts between the national employee representatives.

On the other hand, there are those not represented in the EWC: the national works councils, shop stewards etc. who remain sceptical about or are just not interested in the EWC. They cannot understand why the EWC is not making a priority of their local concerns, and in this respect they cannot see what good the EWC can bring. This applies in a much stronger sense to the employees from each country as well. The EWC is not accepted at all at the workplace level. This is clearly a very serious problem of nearly all EWCs which we do not want to go into here.

On the other hand, during the merger process the EWC was clearly successful in being accepted by management, even if strategic and tactical reasons may have been behind this development. We explained that the management tried to integrate the EWC into the merger as a kind of mediator, with the intention of using the EWC to convey the merger to national employee representatives and the workforce and in order to avoid possible resistance from them and the EWC. This is the reason for using the term "functionalising" of the EWC.

The EWC is able, if it acts shrewdly, to put forward demands and express both its own concerns as well as those of employees, even if management mainly sees it in terms of how they can use it for their own purposes. As mentioned earlier, this view may be elaborated further.

Case Study 2:[19] The European Works Council of Electrolux-Zanussi within the re-structuring process of the company

Concept and aim of the case study

The "Electrolux-Zanussi" EWC is of special interest in two respects in terms of the Europeanisation of industrial relations, especially with regard to the interactive effects between the national and the European levels:

- Zanussi is one of the leading companies in the development of participative industrial relations in the works council and at company level. Of all the participation systems that were implemented in Italy during the past 15 years, Zanussi's model is not only the oldest, but also without doubt the most developed and regulated most strictly by the conditions of collective agreements. This is shown by the setting-up of a committee, similar to a supervisory board ("consiglio di sorveglianza") in 1996. This was a very significant new development for a national system of industrial relations that was generally characterised as an "antagonistic model". It can be expected that the new participative institution of the European Works Council will operate in more favourable conditions at Zanussi - in contrast to the rather marginal way it has been treated by most Italian companies. The manner and fashion how the EWC will integrate into the existing and quite dense network of information and consultation committees and which connections will be made is one of the central questions of this case study. This allows us to investigate the thesis that European developments are strengthening the "participative development" of industrial relations in Italy.
- The other reason for a case study on Electrolux-Zanussi is the central role that the European Works Council was given by the company management within the framework of re-structuring plans announced in 1997. In contrast to the Renault-Vilvoorde case and in order to avoid a similar outcome, the EWC soon became the central location for information exchange within the company. We will also take a closer look at the dynamics and the results at national level and the transnational trade union network.

---

[19] The empirical survey was performed by Ingrid Artus, Bruno Cattero, Christian Dufour, and Adelheid Hege. The case study by Bruno Cattero was slightly edited and cut and provided with a final paragraph (Conclusion) by the team from Bremen.

The Electrolux Group of Companies

Electrolux - a global player in a globalised sector Electrolux, the Swedish company owned by the Wallenberg family operates world-wide and produces electric appliances. Its main competitor for world market leadership is the American Whirlpool Group. Electrolux is the market leader in Europe (albeit not Western Europe - Bosch-Siemens leads the market here). It has production facilities in 22 countries, not only in EU member states, with a total of 56,000 employees (table 5.1 lists the countries represented in the EWC). World-wide, Electrolux employs approx. 105,000 persons in 160 countries.

Table 5.1 Electrolux in Europe: Production units and largest warehouses respective distribution facilities (1998)

Country	Sites/ Distribution	Employees	
		Workers	Total
Italy	18	10177	11887
Sweden	21	6765	8794
Germany	10	6105	7416
Hungary	4	2777	3161
Great Britain	4	2176	2851
Spain	6	2128	2583
France	12	1463	2068
Denmark	6	681	989
Austria	2	560	808
Switzerland	4	413	619
Norway	3	235	305
Total:	90	33480	41481

Source: Electrolux

Electrolux owns subsidiaries and well-known brands in certain countries, e.g. AEG in Germany, or Zanussi in Italy. The company reflects the strong tendency to concentration characteristic of the European "white goods" industry (electrical household appliances), no independent British, French or Spanish producer has survived this process. Market share in Western Europe - with about 25% still one of the largest sales markets - is fiercely fought for by a relatively small number of companies, among them the American white goods manufacturer, Whirlpool. In terms of products the most important countries within the EU are Germany (32% of the EU output), Italy, France, the UK and Spain.

Apart from the concentration process, there are two more structural characteristics of the industry which are of special importance: standardisation of production - mainly the new 'platform strategy' - and the immense increase in productivity:

> The manufacture of electrical household appliances involved mass production with a high degree of standardisation. Approx. 60% of the base materials and components used in the production of electrical appliances are standardised (Panorama der EU-Industrie 97, p. 13-68). Meanwhile, the electrical appliances industry underwent a second process of standardisation : The industry increasingly makes use of the so-called "platform strategy", i.e. the production and rationalisation technology, developed by the automotive industry is transferred to the production conditions of electrical household appliances. By using standard elements, i.e. parts that can be used for all products, and system parts, i.e. parts that are specific to the individual product type and are used for product differentiation, massive reductions in the production costs are achieved. ... This has a negative impact on employment rationalisation . ... This produces another boost in productivity. In 1997, productivity increased by 7.9%, in 1998 by another 3.2% (per employee hour) (IG Metall 1999, pp. 7-8).

Coupled with stagnating or even decreasing demand due to the high degree of market saturation in the industrialised countries, continuing rationalisation has had a significant negative effect on employment: employment in Germany has fallen by 13.4% since 1995 (IG Metall, 1999, p. 15). Staff reductions remained the central focus of the rationalisation policy of Electrolux.

Electrolux in Italy: Zanussi

Company structure Zanussi is a former family-owned company with headquarters in Pordenone in North-Eastern Italy, a region where quite a few of the 18 Italian plants are located. Just like the other Italian household appliance manufacturers, Electrolux's production facilities are traditionally located in rural areas with an agricultural background and no worker's tradition at all; up to the seventies, production facilities were run in the traditional Italian paternalistic style. During the sixties and seventies, Zanussi acquired the Italian companies Castor and Zoppas. In 1973, the first connection with AEG was established when AEG acquired 20% of Zanussi. The attempt to establish itself independently on the European market ended in 1984 with Zanussi's take-over by Electrolux. Within the company group, Zanussi produces the entire product range of electric household appliances (dish-washers, washing machines, dryers, refrigerators, kitchen ranges), including components such as compressors and motors for compressors. In addition, the company manufactures machines and installations for commercial use and vendomats. In 1998, Zanussi employed 12,000 people.

Within the group, Zanussi has developed into an established power through successful reorganisation and good financial results: The Zanussi management in Prodenone/Porcia is responsible for the entire washing machine division. The strong position of the Italian management is reflected in the latest reorganisation of the European structure. Electrolux has restructured the "white goods" division, creating "Home Products Europe" (HPE) in line with European regions and only 7 top managers are responsible for the entire business unit: 3 from Sweden, 3 from Italy, and 1 from the UK.

Industrial relations - the "Zanussi Model" Whether the significant role of the Italian management within the group has anything to do with the good reputation of the system of industrial relations encouraged and administered by the management, is not dealt with here. Industrial relations at Zanussi are seen in Italy as a very successful model of a "participation system" in terms of collective bargaining at the workplace and, more recently, at company/corporate level as well. The model's origins date back to the mid eighties when Italian industrial relations and most of all, the trade unions, were still shell-shocked by the defeat of the Fiat strike in October 1980 - and Fiat was then seen as an exemplary model of a conflict-free - because union-free - company. In 1985 a group of former Fiat managers, now with Zanussi, moved towards an alternative way of avoiding and eliminating conflict by integrating the trade unions into a system involving participation for parity-defined information and consultation committees at company level. The model developed gradually - not without conflicts with and within the trade unions - on the basis of collective agreements with the trade unions; on July 27th, 1997, the "Testo Unico sul Sistema di Relazioni Industriali e di partecipazione" - a kind of company constitution - was signed that finally set out the spirit and methods of participation for the Zanussi group.

The "Zanussi Model" in its own comprehensive regulations found in the Testo Unico is based on five related sub-systems of information, consultation, negotiation, monitoring and supervision. The general information system extends the contractual right to information, introduced in Italy in 1976, with the right structure according to national (company) and regional (plant-specific) level.

The focus of the entire system is the dense network of joint committees at the company and/or entrepreneurial level, where the latter serve as "contacts" and co-ordinators of the committees of the same name at company level. The decision-making process of the committees is notable for its equal representation and requiring decisions that must be made by a unanimous vote. The procedures of the "special committee for work" are especially complex. This has more influence on the work design and working conditions due to its broader range of tasks than other committees. The president of the special committee is elected and appointed by external experts of the workers' organisations resp. organisation development. He plays the role of primus inter pares in case of opposed opinions between management and worker representatives of interests.

Although such a committee is itself unprecedented in Italian industrial relations, it is the "Supervisory Board" and the "Guarantee Committee" that really establish the "Zanussi participation system" as a model arrangement (Figure 5.2). The "Supervisory Board" (direct translation from consiglio di sorveglianza), first established in 1995, has a rather symbolic function and name obviously alludes to the "German model" as reflected in the title of a short report "Mitbestimmung all'italliana", ("Mitbestimmung" is the German term for co-determination) in the publication "Die Mitbestimmung (no. 7, 8/1996). The committee only has information and consultation rights and is more like an economic committee.[20] This was the first time that such a committee had been established in an Italian company. The guarantee committee and its composition are also noteworthy (the current chairman is a professor of labour law), as are the sanctions that it can impose and that are supposed to strengthen and formalise the mutual commitments on which the entire system is based.

---

[20] Insofar it would be inappropriate to distinguish between "Co-determination" on the company/corporate level and "Participation" on the plant level. This is not really about the transfer of "German categories" to another country, but about the difference in quality between rights of information, consultation and co-determination. The "Zanussi Model" remains a - quite "rich" - system of information and consultation. This puts the vague statement of the Zanussi management in favour of the European company (comp. Mondini, 1999) into perspective, as it does not answer the question, for *which* regulation the management stands. The Zanussi form of regulation extends the rights of the European Works Council and therefore it can not be taken as a "model" for the European company (more information: Cattero, 1999).

> - "Supervisory Board" (Consiglio di Sorveglianza)
>   Information and consultation about company results and strategies. Only trade union members. Appointment of 3 members by the national boards of FIOM, FIM, and UILM and of 3 members by the trade union co-ordination committee on the management side.
> - Guarantee Committee (Commissione nazionale di garanzia)
>   Composition: External chairman as primus inter pares. Job:
>   - Judging over violations of the duties laid down in the participation system (unilateral decisions during a process, violation of confidentiality, withholding of information etc.)
>   - Verifying of the decisions of the participating committees;
>   - Interpretation problems;
>   Appointment: One of the two parties, works management, individual RSU -unified trade union committee.
>   The Guarantee Committee is empowered to impose sanctions:
>   - RSU: Reduction of free periods;
>   - Trade unions: Reduction of fees (minimum one month);
>   - Company: Fine (trade union fee of one month).
>   Contributions or fines paid go into a fund set up to cover the costs of the Guarantee Committee.

Figure 5.2 Zanussi: Consultation and controlling committees (Company Level)

Source: Gruppo Electrolux-Zanussi (1997)

In conclusion, the Zanussi system represents an attempt to harmonise participation and negotiation. The participation is based on and supported by contractual negotiations but is strictly separated from them: Problems that can not be solved via the countless possibilities for participation may become the focus of "traditional" negotiations. The participation system definitely tries to "freeze" conflict - every conflict has to be dealt with by the relevant committees first, complying with the 15-day "peace obligation" and handled in such a way that further negotiations are not required.

This specific aspect of the system was the reason for a recurring conflict within the trade unions during the passing of the "Testo Unico". This was not just connected to the "ideological reservations" of the left wing of FIOM-CGIL (edited, Namuth, 1999, p. 51), but there is a wider problem involved; the role of the elected committee (RSU) at workplace level within the participation system. The system is not based on workplace representation but depends on management combined with external trade unions appointing the members. To some extent this undermines the democratic legitimacy and responsibility of the RSU and represents the negative side of the Zanussi system.

It is hard to say to what extent the system has already been undermined. Although there has been 15 years of workforce participation at Zanussi, there are no empirical surveys into how it has worked and whether it has produced any concrete results. The detail and language of the "Testo Unico" create - even with declared supporters of participation - the impression that it is 'more a legal entity than an effective and mature participation structure' (Baglioni, 1998, p. 54).

The re-structuring plan from 1997 and the "International Auction" In April 1997 there was a change in management at Electrolux. On June 12th of that year, during a press conference the new management announced a comprehensive re-structuring plan. At the same time, an extraordinary meeting of the European Works Council was convened for mid-July with the same central topic. The world-wide re-structuring plan involved:

- loss of 12,000 jobs;
- closure of 25 production facilities;
- closure of 50 warehouses.

The main argument for these measures was low profitability: The return on capital was 6 to 7%, instead of the expected and targeted 15% (cf. IG Metall, 1999).

The background of the re-structuring plan was (Alpha Group et al., 1997; Delaunay, 1998):

- After the successful years (1992 to 1995) with growing markets and increasing demand, mainly in Eastern Europe, Asia and South America, a negative trend emerges, primarily due to increasing pressure from the American competitor Whirlpool, that began in 1994.
- The Western European market, long-since saturated, is stagnating.
- At the same time, the Electrolux product range shows a very distinct and - according to the management - "excessive" product distinction according to the national model and one had neglected to look at the "price of distinction".

Within the context of the new and successful "platform concept" mentioned above, the new goal is now to re-centralise and standardise production.

The point of reference in the strategy and organisation of Electrolux is successful competitor Whirlpool: One plant, one (standardised) product, one location. It is not yet clear whether there is any dispute about the background, arguments and goals of the plan.

A 1997 report (Alpha Group), partly invalidated and questioned the arguments and goals. As a result there was a need for an "economic consultation" by the European Works Council, covering freedom for solid concepts and implementation of the plan. It is a fact that the conglomerate's management took care that the "pressure to globalise" was appreciated by everybody right from the beginning:

> If this was only about satisfying the needs of a family, one could do without [re-structuring]. The Wallenbergs could very well accept medium to long-term planning. But the American pension funds require results - otherwise they will invest their capital elsewhere (Gian Marion Rossignolo, chairman of the Board of Zanussi).[21]

The Europeanisation of industrial relations at Electrolux - site competition and trade union nationalism

The EWC at Electrolux - three "Trade union cultures" The European Works Council at Electrolux was set up in 1995 after 3 years of negotiations. It meets once a year. The only exception to this was in 1997 when an extraordinary meeting was convened because of the company's re-structuring plan.

The EWC is composed of 25 members, among them two experts from the trade union side (currently one Swedish expert from the Swedish union LO and one from the EMF) who only take part in the preparatory meetings. Sweden, Italy and Germany - the three core countries according to the persons interviewed in Italy - have three seats each, although Sweden has another four trade union representatives on the Supervisory Board. The other countries are "satellites" of these three core countries - according to those interviewed - 'the Scandinavian countries, (Norway, Denmark) are related to Sweden, Austria is connected to Germany, and Belgium is connected with Italy'. The latter, rather surprising, link has its origin in the Italian descent of the Belgian

---

[21] Excerpt from an article in L'Unita from June 6th, 1997, with the title: "Zanussi [says] to the Unions: Beware - we could leave Italy!".

worker's representative. Hitherto, the French have played only a minor role or no role at all.

> You hardly see them at all and we cannot do anything, because the appointment of EWC members is a national affair.

Until 1998 the French workforce was "represented" by a delegate from the CGT. Since the CFDT has become the majority trade union, it holds the EWC seat.

The non-EU countries, Switzerland, Hungary and Romania, are also represented in the EWC. Despite this positive feature, this is not considered to be a model agreement. "Consultation" is not on the agenda at all and there are no binding and specific instructions about timing and content of the information to be provided. Until July 1997, it was all about very formal meetings, the same also applied to the steering group, which is composed of three worker representatives and three representatives of the management. Although it meets every four months, the steering group is mostly busy with the bureaucratic organisation of the annual EWC meeting.

National employee representatives and the EWC within the context of the company re-structuring

An extraordinary EWC meeting was convened in mid-July (after the press announcement), a two-day meeting took place in October 1997. The company's strategy was not to announce a unilateral decision, but just to set out the economic situation, the "inherent necessities" of restructuring and to mention the sites most affected by this. The potential closure of these sites depended on their ability to implement convincing measures to increase productivity and cut costs. A "comparison" between plants was to decide the outcome - from the trade union point of view this is tantamount to an "international auction" and as such unacceptable and had to be rejected.[22]

The trade unions, however, did not succeed in putting up a joint resistance or agreeing on a common strategy. The company's strategy, to pinpoint "scape goats" or "necessary sacrifices" all over Europe, not only did not lead to any trade union solidarity of any kind, but to the contrary: the competition between the sites, (provoked by management) became a trade union competition - in management terms: "a competition between national systems of industrial relations". At the

---

[22] So Gaetano Sateriale from FIOM CGIL, a dedicated supporter of the Zanussi Model who has to fight against resistance within his own organisation.

end of the process, among the losers were the U.K., where one plant was closed, and Sweden, where the trade unions failed to save the Aligsäs site. On the winner's side was Italy: even if some sites were on the red list for closure, all of them were in a position to be saved.[23]

This is the result of the national fragmentation of trade union activity and the activities of the workplace representatives. Communication and mutual exchanges of information were generally inadequate, with slight differences between the national workplace representatives which we do not want to list in more detail here.

Even the EWC could not cope with this shortcoming, although the steering group was meeting on a monthly basis:

> It was quite difficult - even in the steering group - to get hold of information from other countries. (...) What's going on is information on the lowest possible level (expert discussion with German representative).

Separated and isolated from each other, trade unions and workplace representatives tried to argue the case for the sites they represented and so inevitably this meant they were in competition with each other. In Spain, the comité de empresa and the company management together turned towards the regional (La Rioja) and the central governments. The central government offered more than 900 million Pesetas to Electrolux in order to get the planned investment for production of a new "Euro-Combi" refrigerator for Spain (against competition from Hungary) including 700 jobs.

> We have to assume that the Spanish option succeeded because of two reasons: Firstly, thanks to the state subsidy compared to the Hungarian alternative and secondly, thanks to the low work-related costs compared to northern European sites. This is what actually happened according to the EIRO correspondent from Spain (EIROnline, Nov. 23rd, 1997).

Even in Germany, the 'Bavarian government exerted a certain amount of pressure' (expert interview with German representative). This leads to the spare parts warehouse (that was supposed to move to Paris, France) being transferred within AEG (from Nuremberg to Rothenburg, Germany). But this was one of few successful results. In 1994 AEG employed 9,000 people, 4,000 of whom were working in Nuremberg. Today, only 2,500 are left at the Nuremberg site. The other 1,500 jobs

---

[23] For the time being - until 1999 - 2000 is seen as a "review year".

were cut back within a 6-month period - which corresponds exactly with the instructions from Sweden:

> As a member of the Works Council you were simply not provided with any room for manoeuvre: It was obvious that Electrolux had decided to push the plan through. A strike under such conditions would have meant suicide, as we were hardly able to influence the number of job cuts at all (expert interview with German representative).

Finally, in Italy the Valloncello site was in direct competition with the Aligsäs site in Sweden, and both, Aligsäs first, were on the list of sites to be closed. Worse still, closing one of the sites meant that production was shifted to the winning site, leading to continuing security of employment.

> The Swedish trade union agreed to take back wage increases already negotiated for the next year in order to increase competitiveness. When Electrolux accepted this offer, the Italians appealed to the Italian Ministry of Industry to ensure compliance with the contracts signed when Zanussi was acquired by Electrolux - thus considerably irritating the Swedish trade union who were accustomed to very strict and free collective bargaining. The Italians on the other side deemed their actions in harmony with their national laws and their lack of trade union solidarity is in their eyes justified by the fact that there was no common trade union strategy from the beginning (Delaunay, 1998).

At the "international auction" - the term used by the Italian trade unions and something they thoroughly disapproved of, they still managed to play a trump card that was at least as good as the home advantage of their Swedish "colleagues": When Electrolux acquired Zanussi in 1984, the company had had to guarantee to the Ministry of Industry that it would not close any Italian sites during the first four to five years and, by means of an extension of this period, not to close any Italian sites later on. In addition, the Italian government committed itself to measures to support innovation in the industry, the binding character of which was secured by the signing of an agreement between Electrolux-Zanussi and the trade unions on December 12th, 1997.

Zanussi's other trump card was just as good: this was the system of participation which had just been saved after a crisis that had developed due to conflicts in the RSU between individual sites, and that had gone as far as to threaten the possible termination of agreements by the management in July of 1997. A major cut in staff would have seriously called into question the sense and purpose of such a system and could have possibly brought it to its knees. On the other hand, without this safety net, re-structuring would not have proceeded without a conflict, which would have undermined any potential reductions in costs. An alternative view is that the range of information provided helped gain acceptance of the need for re-structuring measures and so the implementation of the agreed measures was not hindered by any disputes (expert interview, management representative Italy).

The collective agreement from December 1997 mentioned above includes quite a few concessions made by the trade unions and they succeeded in limiting the staff cuts to 374. The Swedish site Aligsäs is now closed.

For Delaunay (1998) the decision in favour of the Italian site is only the first step, because Electrolux is slowly retreating from a European market, which is more or less saturated. Future strategies focus on Eastern Europe where the market is still open and the competition (e.g. Whirlpool in the Czech Republic) is already active. At the same time, wages are low and plenty of workers are available. And Romania, too, would love to be the location for mass production as it could take over the role that Italy had played as an important site for the production of kitchen appliances.

These dark prophecies do not yet really correspond to what is actually happening, but new and worrying developments were to be noted even before the "review year of 2000". So, we assume, Electrolux is now going to outsource component production (pumps, compressors, motors) and set-up individual and independent companies. In Italy alone this would affect five sites with a total of 3,000 employees. It seems uncertain if not doubtful whether they will still be part of the system of participation of Zanussi when they are new companies no longer belonging to the Electrolux conglomerate. They will most certainly not profit from the advantages of a possible extension of the guarantees covering the Italian sites. The result of competition between sites and trade unions - a Pyrrhic victory?

Italian trade unionists are well aware of the reverse side of their own victory, most of all the closure of the Swedish site Aligsäs. Conclusions, drawn shortly after the end of the negotiations were that:

> The Electrolux negotiations have clearly shown at least some of the limitations of trade union action at European level which need to be addressed. Identifying just the most important ones; it does not make any sense to approach a multinational company with such a variety of bargaining arrangements and systems of representation; the EWC should limit itself to its right to monitor company information; trade unions need to co-ordinate their individual bargaining strategies; the

Italian procedures based on co-determination (codecisione) and consultation seem to be the best way of confronting the logic of globalisation. There is a lot to be done, even for the Italian trade union movement. As little has been invested into the trade unionists' Europe it was not possible to completely present the country's own connections and negotiation models. ... There is a European challenge, even for the participation system at Zanussi that represents an opportunity to encourage a culture and practices that will not be able to survive as a solitary entity (Sateriale, 1998, pp.398-99).

Our results show that all representatives have a regional view of conflicts in trade union policy. How did the national representatives perceive the EWC's role within the re-structuring process and how do they generally value the EWC's situation and prospects?

The role of the EWC within the re-structuring process assessment of the national participants

France "Europeanisation" remains an abstract term at the French site and few people know what it means. In addition, there had not been any opportunity to meet trade union colleagues from other countries. A CFDT representative from another site had talked with the French EWC delegate but contact with him is infrequent and so information did not reach him. This shortcoming can not be traced back to the question of which organisation he was a member of as the discussion partners belonged to the CFDT. Furthermore, there is never any direct contact with competing sites within the company because no one knew which sites were potential competitors. The language barrier was a 'really big problem'. Additionally, 'more information was provided on the level of the French comité de groupe than on the European level'. In terms of the re-structuring measures, the EWC did not play 'any role' at all as it was not involved in negotiations and was 'utterly powerless' to influence any decisions which were made. Interventions of any kind could only occur at workplace level and would have to proceed from the local trade union structures.

Germany The internal flow of information when considering the overlapping functions of the same individual (in this case the chairman of the German general works council GWC) on the work of the EWC and the steering group presents no problem at all in Germany:

Official reports are distributed during GWC meetings and you can meet all the key people - at least with regard to the Nuremberg site - on an almost daily basis. But this still does not help improve the transnational flow of information. The problem in this case has nothing to do with language, but with the fact that people are not interested in the exchange of information: 'The Swedes are not prepared to co-operate' and it has been years since a reply from Italy. Disappointed by all this, the German representatives have a deeply negative assessment: The EWC is considered "helpless" and they have very low expectations about it.

Italy Italian worker representatives consider the EWC as a place to get information on the conglomerate - 'information of entrepreneurial character. Trade union topics are not dealt with at all'. In trade union terms the EWC is portrayed as a foreign body, nobody knows what to do with. Firstly, the EWC members are currently not interested in matters to be discussed in the EWC: 'There is no feedback for the steering group'. In order to solve this problem, questionnaires have been distributed (for the second time already) but only 7 of the 25 contacted (deadline end of April) had responded by mid-June.

The exchange of information is still fragmentary and informal. A joint week of further training in London did not produce any obvious improvements.[24] Even within the Italian delegation (three representatives) formal contacts and exchange of information had only just occurred:

> It is only a month since regular meetings have been held with the intention of discussing the current steering group agenda beforehand (expert interview, Italian representative).

The intention is to optimise EWC work and its effects, even if the three Italian EWC members are bound to meet with considerable resistance "at home".

The full-time Zanussi consultant of one of the three metal trade unions in Pordenone (Zanussi's headquarters) says quite freely - the support of the external trade union 'will not be granted as the trade union still acts and thinks on a national level'. From this point of view 'the European Works Council is a group of people that are called together by the Big Boss'.

> I have information on the work of EWC because my delegate - who is also a member of the local executive committee of the organisation - is right here in Pordenone. If he worked at another site, I would not know a thing about it.

---

[24] Topics during the week were structure and organisation of the company, economic conditions, and information on group and company level as well as different systems of industrial relations.

If information and communication depends on individual contacts not only between organisations but also within an organisation it is no wonder that

> nobody will call a German to tell him: 'Look, we are currently discussing such and such problem. How is the situation at your plant?' The principle or belief is still maintained that information is power or, at least, a privilege. This applies locally as well as nationally. In 1997, during the restructuring, nobody would have dreamt of informing the Germans or Swedes about the negotiations here. And this applies to us in Italy too. Nobody from Rome ever thought it would be of any use to call his EWC representative and ask him to provide some information on the current rumours about the outsourcing of component production from Electrolux. They [the national trade unions] call the top management and get their information directly. People think in "territories" and in "organisations". There is competition for information and nobody ever thinks of passing it on (expert interview, Italian trade union secretary).

An additional difficulty resulted from the lack of a feeling of solidarity within Zanussi and between RSU members in the same organisation. The only moment of solidarity was the renewal of the collective agreement. Otherwise it is:

> If I asked a delegate about how often he had called other delegates of his organisation, 90% would give one and the same answer: Never! (ibid.).

In addition, workers are not aware of who is on the EWC:

> The other RSU and the organisation forget that I am a member of the EWC. If I wanted to pass on information I would not know who to turn to, I simply do not know who is interested. The proximity to other RSU is there - physically - but not mentally. For them, Electrolux is too far away (expert interview, Italian representative).

This situation is made more difficult by the fact that the Italian representatives within the EWC are not elected by the RSU committee but by individual organisations. There is only a formal communiqué from the trade union concerned to the trade union RSU committee (coordinamento RSU).

> What is missing is an appreciation on the basis of clearly defined rules which can not be the appointments which are common practice today. Otherwise, the EWC members have no authority who they are obliged to and who they feel committed to. Currently, we find ourselves in a paradoxical situation as it is formally not planned that the

> representatives in the EWC automatically belong to the "coordinamento RSU". Of course, they take part in all meetings but then, anybody could ask: 'What are you doing here?' (expert interview, Italian trade union secretary).

This illustrates why the flow of information within the EWC, at least from Italy, does not work nor does it achieve anything. This is aggravated by the fact that the EWC's own work is not provided with an appropriate time schedule and that there are no full-time RSU with paid time-off in Italian companies - not even at Zanussi, where information, consultation and participation are fully recognised.

There remains the basic question with regard to demand and how the "Zanussi model" works in practice. Our results support the reservations of those, who argue that there is a gap between the model and reality (Carrieri, 1998).

It is against this background that the following statements and intentions of the Italian Zanussi management - somewhat unusual for Italy - can be understood. The management representative who we interviewed says that the shortcomings of the Electrolux European Works Council stem from the fact that - except for the countries with long trade union traditions - there are

> almost no real trade unionists. Those representing the workforce's interests are poorly prepared, you always have to encourage them and directly ask them to take part in the discussion.

People on the committee and most of all on the steering group would definitely prefer to be dealing with the same people with whom they could jointly and co-operatively direct the developments - 'our participation system is rather one of "co-management" or "co-leading" [cogoverno] than a "co-determination system" - in Italy'. However, such an arrangement is not feasible at the moment, as the leading national Italian officials do not meet the requirement of the EWC agreement, that they should be employees of the company. For this reason, a campaign of persuasion and argument was started within the company. Reservation and resistance will probably be largest on the trade union side. Disputes regarding the re-structuring plan have left deep scars and they certainly have not assisted in the building of confidence.[25]

After the events of 1997/98 the Electrolux EWC has considerably increased its importance 'as centre for co-ordinating flow of information

---

[25] A very few months before the interviews Swedish unionists had flown to Italy in order to check personally if the Italian data on the productivity of the Italian plants were correct.

on finding solutions to problems'. That increased importance has nothing to do with the EWC, but with the steering committee whose goal is "Zanussi-isation". One intends to 'invest in the committee' and currently - at least from the Italian side - conceding additional time-off exclusively for those EWC members, active at this level.

All things considered, the Electrolux case is paradoxical. In terms of the three "main core countries" Sweden, Germany, and Italy, it is neither a mixture nor one national culture or form of industrial relations that gains the upper hand. What can be observed is a "Frenchification" of the European Works Council where the management undoubtedly is the more active and strategic player.

Conclusion: The fragmentation of the employee representatives on national lines

In order to achieve a comprehensive assessment of this case, we have to use the scheme of the complex relational network of the EWC described above. This scheme tells us that the EWC is located within a mutual network of tensions between national representatives, the workforce itself, the management, and the trade unions. The EWC has to operate in this complex world with limited powers. This means that the EWC is only able to develop effective working arrangements if it is accepted by the organisations involved, if it provides for a mutual exchange of information, and at the same time develops a clear idea of what it should do. This mainly concerns coming up with its own view of itself as an EWC, solving problems related to internal and external communication and information problems of the EWC, and developing a strategy that forms the basis for its activities.

If we relate the general connections to the very concrete case of restructuring at Electrolux it can be observed that the EWC failed - both internally and externally - to establish a working communications network and to develop a clear idea of what it should be about. This is characterised by the statement of one our interviewees, who said that there is no real interest amongst the EWC members themselves in what to choose as a discussion topic for the EWC. The exchange of information is still fragmentary and it seems that it is not even systematically organised within the national delegations themselves, as reports from Italy revealed. Only recently, and just before our study commenced, was an attempt made at systematically establishing information procedures. Additionally in Italy - and probably in other countries as well - no special time-off is assigned to the EWC work. Moreover, the EWC sees the impact of three different "trade union cultures among worker representatives" between which any approach or communication is very difficult.

With this in mind, it is no surprise that the EWC did not have its own strategy, and that it subsequently could not affect or prevent the "international auction" deliberately launched by the Electrolux management.

Of course, this is not only the fault of the gaps in the EWC's activities but also the result of the way that representatives in each country work and think. Subsequently "Europeanisation" is an abstract term for the French representatives interviewed. There was no opportunity to meet with trade union colleagues from other countries and information about the work of the committee is rare. As for the rest, 'more information is passed-on at the level of the French comité de groupe than at the European level'. With regard to the restructuring measures, the European Works Council did not 'play a role at all' as it is not a place to negotiate. People were 'utterly powerless' to influence any decisions. Intervention of any kind could only occur at workplace level and would have to work through the local trade union structures.

In Germany, people consider the European Works Council as more or less "helpless" and the impression is given that an exchange of information is not really wanted. The language barrier is also very important.

In Italy, the EWC is considered an institution for providing information about the company's management and the EWC is perceived as a foreign body, nobody knows what to do with.

During the restructuring process, the worker representatives (plant-specific and/or trade union) acted separately from each other, in an isolated manner, - so much that the EWC was too weak to compensate for. The weakness itself was the result of the fact that the EWC was to a large extent ignored by the worker representatives/trade unions and was also due to the poor flow of information. In several countries (Spain, Germany, Italy) the EWC was ignored to such an extent that state institutions had to be brought in to represent national site interests instead of attempting a common and unified approach against the conglomerate management via the EWC.

From the point of view of the worker representatives and trade unions, the situation reveals an EWC that is more or less ignored and a national fragmentation of worker representatives, a fragmentation that is directly linked to the poor performance of the EWC.

However, what is behind the connection between the EWC and the Electrolux management that actively and officially integrated the EWC into the restructuring process? This was a direct attempt by management to use the EWC and has nothing to do with it really accepting the EWC as an independent committee. If Electrolux's strategy worked well this is due not so much to the EWC's mediation and conciliation but to each country putting the interest of their plants first encouraged by the company management and the fragmentation of workplace representation - neither of which could be counteracted by the EWC.

The Electrolux management is obviously no longer interested in relying on strengthening the steering committee and its parity composition but on the EWC as a committee of the entity.

The workplace representatives have to suspect that this set-up described will - in the medium term - not work to the advantage of any of the countries concerned.

Case Study 3:[26] The European Works Council of ABC between national and European interests

Concept and aim of the case study

For several reasons the case of the ABC European Works Council is of considerable interest when assessing the tensions between the European and national levels of industrial relations. The case reflects a quite contrary situation in these tensions:

- the expansion of the European Works Council is closely connected to the decrease in importance of national worker representation at the conglomerate level. It was a conscious decision to strengthen the central committee and increase its responsibilities and resources, and to dispense with the stronger de-central and Europe wide co-ordination approaches.
- here the French trade unions competing at national level could - at least in some areas - overcome their differences in order to ensure a co-ordinated and representative approach within the European Works Council.
- the French national and workplace representatives try to use the European Works Council as a platform in order to make their workplace-specific problems the concerns of the entire European

---

[26] The empirical survey for this case study was done by Ingrid Artus, Christian Dufour, and Adelheid Hege (IRES/Paris). The case study was written by Ingrid Artus and slightly edited and cut. As opposed to the other case studies, the statements in this study are largely anonymous in order to prevent the possibility of them being attributed to the individuals who made them. This inevitably undermines the impact of the case study.

committee. This creates a dilemma for the EWC's European experts that is solved by excluding the conflict from the area of responsibilities of the Europe-wide representation.

The report below is largely based on the evaluation of the corresponding expert literature, a range of company documents and statistical data from France, Italy, and Germany, as well as on the observations of EWC meetings, and several expert interviews in France, Italy, Germany, and Belgium (between May and September 1999).

The conglomerate ABC

History, structure and relevant data   ABC is a manufacturing conglomerate which operates worldwide. Although worldwide, ABC is a true "European company". The "European company identity" (as it is presented to outsiders by management) is confirmed by its economic results: in 1998 approx. 75% of the turnover was generated in Europe, more than 60% of which was in EU countries. Other key focal points of entrepreneurial activity are North America and - starting-up a few years ago - South East Asia (mainly China and Thailand).

In 1998, the group's economic situation was stagnant. The "disappointing" results of 1998 according to the management, were due to operations in Eastern Europe (Poland, Hungary, Ukraine, Russia) where 'people were still working at adjusting the prices to the market's possibilities' (interview with the management).

ABC's activities are organised into five sectors of production.
Company D with 4,500 employees was the focus of this case study. At the end of 1998, ABC had almost 22,000 employees. Approx. 18,000 employees worked in European companies, 13,000 of them within the EU. France and Italy are the main centres of the group's activities, followed by Poland, Spain, Hungary, Germany, The Netherlands, and the U.K.

Company D in France - the specific regional nature of employee representation at plant level

The company D's activities are co-ordinated from its headquarters in Belgium. Larger sites are located in France, Italy, the UK, Germany, Belgium and The Netherlands. North America is another key area in terms of production and employee numbers. After turnover and profits decreased in 1997 company D saw a significant increase in turnover and profits in 1998, although this was largely due to results in the USA. At the end of

1998 the number of D employees world-wide was approx. 4,500 and little changed from 1997.

D's only French production site is located in a rural area in Northern France. The administration, including the personnel and other departments, and the management is separated from the production plant in Northern France and located within another company site.

The situation of the employees and their representatives in D's French production plant could be described as "island like" in two ways:

Firstly, the company is a kind of "regional stronghold" in terms of wages and working conditions which are significantly above average for the area. For example, there is an extensive - and for the employees pretty lucrative - bonus system for week-end and shift work in the all-shift system. Wages are significantly higher than in agreements. While wages in many of the region's plants have fallen to the legal minimum (SMIC), D's employees earn close to double (on average) and the legal minimum wage is not applied. There are very few limited or other precarious employment contracts. Working time has been cut down to 37.5 hours for some time now and currently negotiations are taking place over a reduction to 36 hours - management's response to the workforce's demand for a 35-hour week.

The good pay and conditions - good at least when seen in the regional context - were achieved, by the 'fact that we went on strike in 1985' according to the secretary of the Comité d'établissement (CE). This was the year when production was changed from semi to all-shift production, resulting in a significant reorganisation of available working time for the employees. The conflict in the company, with approx. 60% in the union at the time, could only be resolved with major financial concessions to the workforce. The new company management, appointed after the strike, played it safe, did not risk any serious disputes and to deal with the workplace representatives' strategy on representation at the plant. With this in mind, the successes of 1985 (in terms of pay and workplace representatives) have been maintained.

The second reason for the "island" character of the plant in Northern France is that people in such a rural area are more or less cut-off from any contact with other workplaces within the company. One of the main reasons for this is the fact that management, with its privileged information, has its headquarters at the administration site far from D's location. The workforce representatives have only one production manager contact who is bound to consult the company management with regard to any crucial topics or bargaining issues. As international contact between D's sites in individual countries is at a managerial level, the site itself is rather isolated from these channels of information. The workforce representatives of D's

French production plant have only had one direct contact with colleagues from other plants of the company (in 1998, during a trade union-organised international meeting). The site still has to rely on the management for information on the working conditions at other sites 'that make interesting comparisons'.

It is not only the management but also ABC's EWC that is remote from events at the Northern French site. Admittedly, four of the EWC representatives come from D's sites in Belgium, Germany, the U.K., and The Netherlands, but there is not really that much contact between them, or between the four French EWC representatives who come from companies in different sectors. The CE secretary does not even have much contact with "his representative" in the EWC who is a trade union representative of a different sector. It is clear that the CE secretary gets his information about the EWC and the conglomerate's development on an European level almost exclusively from the management.

All in all, the case proves that the range of action available to any workplace representative is structured according to regional and national conditions.

Work conditions on-site, regional competition, the labour market, the degree of trade union organisation within the plant, and workforce's potential to mobilise, are all determining factors in establishing the critical parameters of worker company representatives in the company. Another important factor is contact with trade union and other national representatives within the plant (e.g. in France: comité de groupe). There is an interest in contacts at the European level - even if it is rather abstract and non-committal - but the general feeling is that one can just as well do without these contacts.

The European Works Council of ABC

The EWC - caught between group-wide employee representation and maintaining trade union influence   Negotiations on establishing a European level representative body for ABC started in 1993. There were three reasons for the conglomerate's decision to establish the EWC: firstly, the basic and most important incentive for action was the European Directive, which was then being drafted by the European Commission. Secondly, while management was considering a pro active move as a way of staying ahead of union demands, several trade union bodies asked management about setting up a groupwide information and representation committee The Italian trade unions, in particular, put forward demands for a discussion forum at group-level, and the French comité de groupe expressed a similar wish. Thirdly, the establishment of a European information committee suited ABC's philosophy in which "social dialogue" plays a crucial and propaganda role in the group's presentation.

> We believe that anticipating negotiations with our social partners offers advantages for both sides (...). The social dialogue is well regarded within the group of companies, and I would say it is a cultural reality (management of ABC).

After the group decided in principle to establish a European representative committee, it appealed to the respective Euro-federation in order to negotiate and sign an agreement with each. Officially, the "conscious decision" in favour of negotiations with the European union federations was justified by the fact 'that our company is European and we wanted to give it a distinctly European colour' (management of ABC). Personal contacts between decision makers within the ABC conglomerate and the officials of the European federations played a decisive role in this process.

It still took 18 months before signing the agreement (on establishing a European Works Council) between the European Trade Union Confederation and the ABC conglomerate in 1995. Two problems had to be solved in order to reach an agreement: firstly, the presidency of the EWC, and secondly the question of which union organisations were to be represented on the new committee.

The European Trade Union Confederation would have preferred to see a workforce representative as the president of the EWC - or at least - a representative of the workforce rotating with a representative of the management. The trade unions did not succeed in winning this argument - according to the ABC negotiator 'characterised by the German culture of co-determination'. The compromise agreed upon finally guaranteed a central role within the new committee for the Euro-federation. While the president of the group of companies is officially also the president of the EWC (so that the central directive power is obviously still with the management) the Euro-federation was allowed a permanent representative within the EWC who 'plays a special role in comparison to the other delegates' (ABC management). According to the wording of the agreement, this representative appoints the secretary of the EWC as well as directing the composition of the EWC delegates, in accordance, though, with the company.

The appointment of a French union member as the secretary of the EWC was therefore initially not based on a democratic election process of any kind, but on an appointment made by the Euro-federation. After the four-year term of office the representative was re-elected by the EWC delegates, legitimising his actions and efforts prior to the re-election.

The second crucial aspect of the negotiations on the EWC was the question of: which French trade unions should be part of the new European committee? This was particularly about representation for the CGT and CGC - two trade unions that are strongly represented within ABC but that were not (at that time) members of the Euro-federation. Ironically and interestingly enough, the representatives of ABC management and the CGT-FO member in particular supported and defended the participation of the CGT as well as the CGC in the new representation structure against the Euro-federation.

To this extent, the "conflicting battle lines" were clearly contrary to the traditional ideological concepts of "labour and capital" or "communism - anti-communism". The dividing line was more between the ABC "company representatives" and the federations "trade union representatives". The question of credibility and representativeness of the new committee was of central importance for the management as well as for the designated secretary of the EWC. In view of the fact that the management declared that the participation of CGT and CGC was a non-negotiable condition and 'the CGT will anyway knock at the EWC's door' (interview ABC management) the Euro-federation finally agreed to give the four French delegate places in the French ABC plants to the four French trade unions.

In total, the new committee was composed of 17 members: 4 French, 4 Italians, 2 Spanish, as well as one delegate each from the UK, Portugal, Denmark, the Netherlands, Belgium, Germany, and Hungary. The participation of the Hungarian delegate was positively received by all concerned as this went beyond the requirements of the European Directive. The "voluntary" admission of the Hungarian representative would tend to enhance ABC's credibility as a 'company interested in pan-European social dialogue'. At the same time, an opening within the European Works Council for a representative from Eastern Europe is simply a question of anticipating expected in future developments.

Four annual meetings have so far been held by the EWC. The conferences were all scheduled for two days, with one day serving as a preparatory meeting for the following one-day official EWC meeting - both days were paid for by the company. In addition, a three-day training seminar was held - also paid for by the company - where economics experts and European Union representatives attended as lecturers. Recently, an EWC Information Bulletin was introduced to all European ABC employees that informs them about the work of the EWC in several languages. Although the introduction of the bulletin is probably an important step toward institutionalising the external representation of the new committee, contact between the committee and the workforce appears to be a shortcoming. There is no formal system for the EWC to spread the information it has obtained to employee representatives at plant/company level (by way of top down reporting) and in the reverse case, there is (with the exception of the comité de groupe in France) no "in-between" body of employee representation that is able to forward information from "bottom to top", i.e. that could gather information from the different ABC sites within one country or within one industry in order to allow the EWC to get a real pan-European overview.

There is therefore the concrete problem that a Portuguese EWC delegate, e.g. coming from a production site, can only profit marginally from information exchange with other delegates coming from completely different industries - and reverse - he himself is not provided with information about the current situation within other Portuguese companies. Internally, this means that mutual information is always of a fragmentary nature and depends somewhat on coincidence; externally, company workforce representatives are not really aware of the relevance of a European representation committee.

The deficits of information exchange do not only concern contact between the committee and the "company base", but also contact between the delegates from different countries.

The importance of a functional flow of information is revealed when we look at a German-Dutch example: the closure of a production site was announced and carried out in Germany. Meanwhile, the same type of production was established in The Netherlands. As both plants were located close to the border of the two countries, it would have been possible for the Dutch unit to employ the laid off German workers, as many of them were living in the Netherlands anyway.

All in all, the ABC case illustrates the fact that pan-European representational committees of this kind always find themselves at the centre of different interests and political areas of influence. It is not only where conglomerate management and workforce representatives interact. Sometimes, the front lines of emerging conflicts spread along the lines of a group's individual workforce representation as opposed to a pan-European Union approach. In the case of ABC, the national and European trade union organisations were able to secure their influence within the EWC to a high degree -with the agreement of the management. In contrast, the legitimacy of the committee as a credible representative forum for the group-wide interests of the workforce seems so far somewhat limited.

The new EWC agreement: strengthening of group-wide European representation versus sector-specific and national representation structures

The EWC agreement, signed in 1995, was a four-year agreement that meant new negotiations would be necessary in spring 1999.

Proposals for reform that were brought forward by workforce representatives on the EWC during the negotiations were focussed on improving the EWC's work rate and making it more professional. The following items were addressed:

- The representatives asked for more frequent meetings (two instead of one). In addition, that the deputy delegates, as well as the delegates, should take part in the meetings.
- Another topic for discussion was the demand for improved resources for the delegates and the definition of substitution rights. These demands are coming from experiences by the EWC and delegates in Spanish and Portuguese plants, not being acknowledged by company management.
- It was demanded that the EWC should be provided with the right to appoint an expert to be paid by the company.
- Finally, during more than one EWC meeting delegates requested that meetings should not only be held on a cross-industry level, but also additional and regular sector-specific meetings should be arranged on an European level. This demand reflects the fact that the five business areas of ABC were operating as profit centres. There are no representatives on the European level from the managing directors resp. directors of human resources of the individual business areas.

The final negotiations resulted in the following organisational reforms:

- The EWC will meet twice a year. Only delegates themselves are admitted to the meetings - plus their deputies from the host country.
- The EWC has the right to nominate an expert.
- A steering committee will be established which will continue the work of the EWC in between the conferences. The steering committee will prepare the agenda of the EWC conferences and will meet when there are problems concerning more than one country. The steering committee is composed of the secretary of the EWC, one member of the ABC management, and the (Italian) representative of the Euro-federation in the EWC plus another

delegate. Depending on the problem in hand, other EWC delegates from the countries concerned may be invited to participate.
- Intensive discussions were held on the question of how to define the terms "information, consultation, and agreement". This discussion resulted in the establishment of an "information calendar" appearing in the new agreement. This implies that the company has to organise a steering committee conference in the event of extraordinary events affecting several countries. The company, before making its decision publicly known, has to inform the steering committee first, during this conference.

At a glance, the new agreement appears to be a success for supporters of the EWC and must be seen as strengthening the workforce's representation at the European level. The rules on information are the key new developments from the trade union point of view. This implies that the agreement will have significant political importance as a model when the EWC Directive is next revised. Without principally questioning this overall assessment, it has to be noted that neither the plan for a representative structure based on the business areas at European level nor increased resources for the EWC delegates were realised in the new agreement. In both cases, the demands, that had been repeatedly put forward by EWC delegates in recent years were not complied with. Agreement on the company's duty to provide information - although just an example - may be of limited practicability and there are doubts as to whether "national" restructuring measures (which do not come under the duty) will always be clearly distinguishable from measures of "international" importance (which do come under the duty). Furthermore, the "information calendar" of ABC appears to be "only" just a listing of rights that already existed. Even from ABC management's point of view, the agreement hardly goes beyond the legal requirements defined by the Vilvoorde conflict. The ABC management representative made it clear that "information" will not mean "co-determination" and "consultation" and will only cover the timing of information and not necessarily result in management consenting to any proposals or demands from the workforce's representatives.

Definitely, the most awkward aspect of the new agreement is not to be found in the official records, but was separately negotiated: The abolition of the French comité de groupe of ABC.[27] The reason behind the

---

[27] In this committee (compulsory in French law) the delegates of those companies of ABC established in France meet on a regular basis. The management is obliged to provide the committee with encompassing information on the economic as well as the employment situation of the group of companies; in addition to that the meetings give the union representatives the opportunity for an information and experience exchange.

agreement is obviously management's demand that the strengthening of employee representation at the European level can only be achieved by accepting the weakening of the national representative structures - a problem concerning France alone as it is the only country that has a significant and group-wide representative structure at the national level. Interviews with the ABC management and an EWC representative clearly showed that the "achievements" of a second annual EWC meeting as well as the permission to appoint an expert for the EWC are a direct exchange for the abolition of the comité de groupe. The ABC management stressed the fact that it would only be able to meet its expanded duties on information and representation at the European level if the "bundle of obligations" that still applied in accordance with the French law was removed. The management wanted to put less effort into a committee that was no longer required because it was established in a time when there were no European structures at all. From the employee representatives' point of view, the right of appointing an expert at the European level seemed to offer the possibility of getting more comprehensive information than at the level of only one single national company site. As the EWC's right to interfere with national French rights was considered to be of a dubious nature, the renunciation of the comité de groupe was not formally laid down in the new EWC agreement.

It seems sensible to see the EWC as a significantly more important body than the comité de groupe when considering the fact that information at European level is really more comprehensive than at the French national level alone (and when we consider the fact that the EWC often represents the unique and sometimes only source of information for those workforce representatives from countries with few trade union rights). On the other hand, this assessment is probably not wholly compatible with the opinion of many French workforce representatives who still consider the national field of action as more important, and who see the comité de groupe as the source of information closer to the company. It remains to be seen what the outcome of this will be because not only European Union approval for the dissolution of the comité de groupe is required but also the approval of the members of the comité de groupe and - at least at the time of the survey - it seemed that this approval would not be forthcoming.

All in all there is a certain ambivalence in the new EWC agreement . On the one hand, it reflects a strengthening of the European level of workforce representation at ABC, and of the continuing consolidation of the EWC as a professionally run institution. On the other hand the foregoing of its national rights of representation is a political issue and the outcome of the initiative is more than uncertain.

The current conflict: using a European body to represent national interests?

During the first meeting of the EWC after the new agreement had been signed, the French delegates announced during the preparatory meeting that they would use the opportunity afforded by the EWC conference to protest against the management's behaviour. On the day of the meeting, they presented the group chairman with a petition of 1,300 signatures and subsequently read out a declaration from the five French trade unions protesting against the management. The French delegates then ostentatiously left the committee. Walkouts were organised concurrently in the French plants.

What were the reasons behind these developments?

The ABC management had decided on a re-structuring plan for a part of the production that was limited to French plants only. This was the reason for major conflict between the French workforce representatives and the management.

This conflict is mainly about three issues:

1. "Re-structuring" the staff will mean that employees will be laid off and/or transferred to other plants.
2. According to the workforce's representatives implementation of the 35-hour week within the frame of the collective agreement of the company, massively infringes on the interests of the workforce as the new round of reduced working hours (from 39 to 35 hours per week) is linked to significant restriction in choice with regard to holiday scheduling and other work-free days. Many employees are not really happy about the fact that the reduction of working hours is linked to the "freezing" of wages for a period of two years.
3. In order to "economise" on costs, the management has decided not to extend resp. change collective bargaining on additional bonus payments for the employees in accordance with company profits. The bonus payments are to be reduced by 70%. Financial losses to the workforce would be significant as bonus payments currently constitute approximately 20% of their entire payment.

All in all, the impact of the re-structuring plan on the French employees is such that employees turned to the "responsible" French management, who informed them that they did not have the power to negotiate.

After being rejected by the French management, the EWC meeting was the only forum (at the time) offering direct contact with the group management - even if this only meant making it forcefully clear that they did not accept the unilaterally decreed plans. This action was explicitly intended as an 'open insult to [the conglomerate management] and not to the European Works Council' and it seemed almost incidental that the EWC meetings served as a stage for it. The ostentatious act of the French delegates, in leaving the EWC, made this a political issue even within the European representation committee, as it very clearly conveyed the message: 'A European dialogue is useless and implausible when the partner of the dialogue refuses to talk at national level and at the same time massively violates the interests of the workforce.'

The situation was characterised by two opposing ideas:

- The delegates were to consider themselves more as European rather than French, in order to allow joint European activities.
- The settlement of national conflicts at the European level serves to generalise a certain form of policy of interests and is therefore suited to advance the "Europeanisation of industrial relations".

The reactions of the other EWC delegates to the company's act were rather disappointing for the French delegates. Informal discussions revealed some international solidarity, but only in the abstract. The Eurofederation stayed neutral.

Conclusion: The European Works Council - part dealing with conflicts at a national level, part keeping its distance from them

To assess this case, we want to use the scheme of complex relationships, as described above, with the European Works Council (EWC) at the centre. This states that the EWC is situated within an interplay of tensions (between the national representatives and the workforce itself, the management and the trade unions).

The EWC has to move within this complex power structure, equipped only with limited authority of its own. It can only develop practical ways of working, if it can be sure of being accepted by the (other) partners, and if it can establish an exchange of information and at the same time come up with a clear idea of what it should be doing. This includes developing an image of itself as an EWC that significantly differs from that of the national representative bodies. This means mastering both the internal and external communication and information problems of the EWC as well as developing a strategy that will help.

In terms of ABC's EWC and the conflict experienced within the committee, there is an obvious clash between the national and European strategies of representative organisations. The case demonstrates at least three different strategies for handling these contradictions:

The "professional European officials" from the national and European trade unions are trying very hard to achieve the "Europeanisation of industrial relations" by establishing close and co-operative contacts between the trade union leaders and the group's management. Bearing in mind the relatively short existence of pan-European committees and management's acceptance of European trade unionism, there is considerable intrinsic value in the existence of co-operative relations. This is the reason to put national-based disputes on a European-level very hesitantly. According to this tendency, this is a strategy of 'strengthening European co-operation by excluding national conflict situations'.

An extreme contrast to this strategy of representation could be seen in the attitude of some of the national trade union officials and plant workforce representatives who hardly attribute any intrinsic value to the European representative organs. They consider the direct representation and protection of the workforce's interests within the plants an urgent priority, and believe that the far-away European representation bodies may be used - from case to case - as a "stage" or "forum". At the same time, the protection of the workforce's interests on plant or national level is considered to be a "conditio sine qua non" for the European dialogue.

The political concept of "strengthening European co-operation by Europeanisation of national conflicts" must be considered just in the middle of these two extremes. Such a strategy is confronted with at least two major problems.

Firstly, there are hardly any organisations/actors, which/who are in a position which would allow the systematic and credible pursuit of such a policy. The European as well as the national trade union organisations are bound to their specific levels and insofar only marginally conditioned for such a policy. Secondly, the strategy of "Europeanisation of industrial relations" is currently limited by the fact that the success of trade union policy always depends on the existence of an "effective" potential of threats and pressure in cases of dispute. The latter exist primarily on national, but hardly on the European level.

All in all, the relationship between the EWC and the ABC management may be described as distinctly co-operative. The management itself promoted the expansion of the EWC at the expense of the national interest representation on a conglomerate level - whatever the reasons for this may have been. Consequently, one should say that the EWC is fully accepted by management.

In conclusion and with regard to the current state of the case presented, it must be noted that - despite the mixture of positive and negative developments for the EWC -for this kind of representative structure , there is still a risk in the fact that they have not really developed a view of what an independent European committee should do. This is why, so far, the employee representatives at ABC had not developed an independent strategy.

Case Study 4: The European Works Council of Kaefer Isoliertechnik and the re-structuring of the company

Concept and aim of the case study

This case study focuses on the re-structuring process at Kaefer Isoliertechnik GmbH during which approximately 50% of employees in Germany were laid-off. We were interested in how the workforce representatives reacted to this and if the Kaefer EWC, set up in 1994, was involved in the negotiation process. At the same time we tried to outline the work of the EWC in order to be able to draw conclusions about its position in the company.

This case study used all company data and publications available. In addition, interviews were conducted in Germany with the chairman and secretary of the EWC, the chairman of the combine works council, the union representative and the human resources manager.

The company Kaefer Isoliertechnik

Kaefer Isoliertechnik is a medium-size company within the construction industry, and is typical of the German "Mittelstand", which goes abroad. Currently, Kaefer has about 1,500 employees in Germany and 1,600 abroad. There are about 20 production sites in Germany. The Kaefer company is represented in 10 European countries (six EU countries as well as Norway, Czech Republic, Hungary, and Poland). Additionally, the company owns sites in South Africa, the United Arabian Emirates, Indonesia, Malaysia and Thailand.

The Kaefer company is a construction service supplier, active as both, main contractor and subcontractor. The company's activities are divided into three business areas:

- construction;
- industry;
- ship building.

The last four years were characterised by comprehensive re-structuring measures within the company. The reasons behind the re-structuring plan are:

1. Change of management as the result of the executive partners retiring and the retirement of the only employed managing partner during 1994 and 1995. The retirement decisions had already been taken in 1993.
2. Critical operational problems during 1992, 1993, and 1994. The year 1994 saw massive losses.
3. Basic market changes/business slump, opening of Eastern markets etc.

The company's position was very difficult at the time, requiring solutions that would ensure the company's continuing existence. Basically two measures were implemented:

- Modification of the organisational structure - away from individual specific sites, and towards the organisation of business areas.
- Reduction of the workforce. This allowed annual savings of about DEM 50 million, with only 25 to 30 million expenditure for the social compensation plan.

In the course of the re-structuring measures, half of the staff in Germany was made redundant (from 3,200 employees in 1994 to 1,500 in 1999). Abroad, staff numbers increased, however, and with a headcount of 1,600, the workforce abroad is now larger than the one in Germany. Turnover in 1994 was approx. DEM 640 million, but fell in following years. Now, turnover has recovered, and is currently almost at the same level as 1994. In order to achieve this, several sites have had to be closed down. Only recently the Dutch and Belgian sites were sold; the buyer of the Dutch and Belgian sites also acquired sites in France.

The reasons for selling both foreign subsidiaries were not only those of economy, but also addressed irregularities in the business practices of the Belgian and Dutch subsidiaries. In the course of the sales process a French site was acquired.

In many instances, closure of sites and reduction of staff was linked with the establishment of individual sub-contractors independent from Kaefer but still working with a certain amount of orders from them. For Kaefer this means outsourcing the entrepreneurial risk. Approximately 150 to 200 of the employees laid-off by Kaefer were transferred in this way to sub-companies.

To a certain extent it is logical (and normal within the construction industry) that the Kaefer company no longer processes all orders itself, but employs sub-contractors. Approximately 60% of the order volume is being processed by Kaefer, the other 40% is awarded to sub-orders. The halving of staff numbers, with only minor losses in turnover, reflects the development of rationalising potential. On the other hand, it illustrates the result of increased sub-contractor use.

The company organisation was fundamentally overhauled in the course of the re-structuring process. At the same time, the management changed. Prior to that, associates were managing partners; today, they are integrated only via the Supervisory Board. The re-structuring was effected after expert opinion had been sought from a management consultant company.

Previously, different sites had been relatively independent, led by the corresponding site management. Today, the company is divided into three business areas that are being managed by the responsible area manager. They report directly to the company management. Site managers are provided with relatively few responsibilities and principally follow the instructions of their respective area managers.

Subsidiary companies abroad belong directly to the limited company. In the past they were independently owned and belonged directly to the Kaefer associates. The subsidiary companies abroad are economically independent units that work for the regional market and do not compete with German sites.

Development, structure and problems of the EWC

The history of the EWC Kaefer set up an EWC as early as 1994, based on a voluntary agreement between the German worker representatives and company management. First initiatives in this direction date back as far as the Eighties. Two years after the introduction of the Single Market in the EU countries, the Works Council of the company formed a committee on the initiative of the German GWC chairman. The committee's task was to implement those changes implied by the introduction of a single European Market, where relevant to the company. In doing so, the worker representative body should be kept working in the face of European integration. At first, interest in this idea from the works council and Unions was low. However, this did not prevent the committee from being installed.

Starting with discussions in the EU committee, initiatives were developed to contact worker representatives within subsidiaries abroad. Massive problems had to be solved during preparations for the first meetings. Finding a relevant contact partner in other countries proved to be especially difficult.

In 1991 the first meeting was held. Even the company managing director was invited to the second meeting a year later. The informal parts of the meetings were used to discuss an idea with the managing director: 'Why not found an EWC?' In the third meeting, this resulted in negotiations with the company management. About five years ago - even before the signing of the directive - an EWC agreement was reached so that the meeting during which the EWC was constituted could be held only a short time later. The meetings were paid for by the EU within the framework of the budget B 4003.

The management had concerned itself little with the EWC issue and therefore did not have any objections with regard to the ideas of the German works council. The managers were of the opinion that it was simply good form for a global company to establish an EWC as the corresponding EU directive was already in preparation. This attitude towards the EWC was to change quite fast when it became clear that any EWC conference was connected with costs to be paid by the company.

There were conflicts with union headquarters in Frankfurt/M., Germany, and Brussels, Belgium, because the agreement did not provide for the inclusion of unionists who did not belong to a company.

The agreement to establish a European Works Council composed only of worker representatives is rather far-reaching. Current affairs as well as preparation and follow-up of the annual EWC meeting are guaranteed by the EWC board consisting of three people. Their jurisdiction extends to the EU countries with the exception of Norway. Union officers not belonging to the company may be engaged as experts by the EWC. The cost of the EWC's work, and the EWC board, is paid by the company. This includes costs for translating documents, travel costs of the chairman to the individual sites etc.. The right of information and the right to be consulted are listed, they include any company relevant developments.

The appointed members of the EWC are responsible for linking the work of the EWC to the individual national worker representative bodies. The German GWC chairman is not a member of the EWC, but he is provided with the right to participate and is supplied with all minutes and aware of all decisions.

The work of the EWC up to the present Initially, the EWC mainly concerned itself with learning about all the EU Directives relevant to the company. The relevant directives and regulations were discussed and worked through during the EWC meetings, in which they looked at management reports. The efforts put into this produced very limited benefits for individual sites. As a result, the EWC asked its members to deal with other issues. This led to the problem of finding new issues for the EWC that were at the same time of direct relevance to the workforce.

Health and safety at work emerged as a suitable subject and is now the central focus of the EWC's work. The overall goal is a company agreement that sets out a common implemented survival policy at all sites. A range of measures is being implemented with the help of the Euro-federation EFBWW, the German union IG Bau as well as EU programmes. A meeting in Brussels is planned next year that will be held over the course of several days and where an attempt will be made to work out a company-wide agreement, which will aim to achieve a higher standard, especially at those sites which currently lag behind.

Overall, it is obvious that the creation of mutual trust between the German works council members and the company management was necessary to get the EWC up and running. The establishment of the EWC was effectively promoted only when a former member of the management participated at a preparatory meeting of worker representatives so making management less suspicious. In addition, this succeeded in establishing a certain trust between the company management and the external union officers, who previously (and traditionally) would have been regarded with scepticism by the Kaefer management.

A similar experience occurred in Austria, where site management at first refused to allow the Austrian works council to co-operate with the EWC. After experiencing an EWC board meeting in Austria (where a personal contact was made) co-operation with the Austrian company management was significantly improved.

The EWC assessed by the participants An evaluation of the work of the EWC has to be carried out in a variety of ways. The main problem for the trade unions is to find topics that have an impact on individual sites. The workplace representatives appeared sceptical as well as optimistic when they were asked about the possibilities for success within the next years. The same applies to the current handling of the main topic, health and safety at work. While some of the interviewees expect stimuli from the Europe-wide agreement to lead to an implementation of higher safety standards within individual sites, there was some scepticism as to whether such an agreement could produce any real results.

There was also some scepticism because of the difficulties in ensuring some continuity in the work of the EWC in some countries. Staff turnover is simply too fast in some EU countries to allow for continuous work, and EWC delegates often change, additionally, some representatives do not show up for meetings, although they have been elected.

On a positive note in some countries the EWC has been able to mediate between workplace representatives and the respective company management at the site. The EWC succeeded in arguing for the interests of the employees.

Considering the results of the EWC work it does not seem surprising that the workplace representatives have very few clear ideas about the EWC's future prospects. There is only consensus on the fact that the EWC will not be signing any collective bargaining agreements in the near future, due to the differing national social and wage systems that exist.

The attitude of the management is quite different: The EWC was established under the old management, where the associates themselves participated to a high degree in management functions. The attitude of the old management was characterised mainly by working to receive the image of a modern and international company.

This motivation is only of secondary importance to the new management. They consider the EWC is superfluous and costly in terms of benefits to the company and basically reject it. Each year, the EWC incurs costs of approx. DEM 60,000 to 80,000. According to management information, this makes necessary a turnover of DEM 600,000 and it is only because of legal regulations that the EWC is still in existence.

Management sees the EWC as inefficient. The same applies to their activities with regard to health and safety, because the problem is not which regulations exist, but if and how they are enforced. This is one of the main problems for countries in Southern Europe and one which can not be solved by Europe-wide agreements. In addition, the subsidiaries abroad are more or less independent. Formally, they have to comply with instructions from the Bremen headquarters, but till now measures demanded by site management abroad have been accepted by the Bremen headquarters, if seen to be economically justified. This also applies to all staff matters. This leads to the assumption that it is the workplace industrial relations in each country that are relevant -and not the EWC.

The EWC's relation to the trade unions There were problems in the course of establishing the EWC, as the EFBWW was not directly integrated into the negotiations. As a result, the EFBWW considered refusing to back the Kaefer company EWC, although the EFBWW was always present or at least informed about any developments. The Kaefer management rejected any negotiations with trade unionists from Brussels because it wanted to avoid becoming "remote-controlled" by Brussels. Meanwhile, the conflicts with the EFBWW have been completely resolved and the quarrel did not result in a permanent disturbance of the relations.

Actually, there is no permanent support from EFBWW or the German union IG BAU with regard to the Kaefer EWC. The system of trade unions within the construction industry provides that the individual EWCs are represented by the trade unions of the country where the corresponding company has its headquarters.

Thus, IG BAU would be responsible in our case, but is not provided with sufficient staff numbers to guarantee the support of medium sized companies such as Kaefer. Currently, attempts are being made to ensure continuing contacts at least with the companies. The responsibilities are to be seized by the existing conglomerate supporters resp. by selected trade union officers as members of the Supervisory Board. Time constraints mean that the secretaries directly imposed by the union headquarters are simply not able to attend to and support individual companies. Their tasks are related to the co-ordination of the work of IG BAU with EFBWW, as well as to the concepts and implementation of Europe-wide trade union activities.

The representation of employees within the re-structuring process   The decision to re-structure the company was made by an inner circle of the management, by 5-8 people, under great economic pressure. A key decision was based on an analysis by an external consulting company. There was no comprehensive concept for various and long-term single measures. All these activities were planned and adapted depending upon the current state of the re-structuring developments. Once management had made a decision, it was implemented through the company hierarchy (top-down approach).

As soon as the company decided on the steps to be taken, the employees concerned, the works council, and the economic committee (institutions set up under the German Works Constitution Act) were informed. The information was released in small entities because among other reasons there was no comprehensive re-structuring plan. The dynamic of the re-structuring process simply developed in single steps and measures as well as through modifications to the external environment. In order to ensure a proper flow of information, some of the representative committees were informed before the affected employees in the different sites.

Social compensation schemes were worked out with the German General Works Council resulting in an approx cost of. DEM 25-30 million. The cost savings resulting from re-structuring were expected to amount to an annual DEM 50 million. This led to some re-thinking on the part of the works council. Prior to that, the Kaefer company had been a successful company. Negotiations with the works council and the company management had mostly been about the distribution of "benefits". This was a painful turning point in the hitherto rather "uneventful" work of the works council that had to be dealt with, and in addition there was the difficult task of mediating the results achieved to the workforce.

The relations between the German General Works Council (GWC) and the company's management in the negotiations were very constructive even if some tensions did arise, which could not be prevented. In the end, this was not only about the reduction of benefits (basically all voluntary social contributions were simply cancelled) but also about the discharging of employees. The German GWC, however, showed some understanding of the fact that the crisis the company found itself in could only be overcome by accepting massive concessions by the workforce. This was the reason why the GWC did not attempt to prevent or hinder the measures the management required, but tried to make the best out of it for the workforce. Today, the constructive relationship continues and has had an impact on current negotiations about a company pension scheme.

The EWC acknowledged the re-structuring process but did not discuss it very extensively. The EWC was not integrated into the negotiations at all. One of the reasons for this was the fact that the number of employees abroad increased, but fell in Germany. The individual sites were affected to quite different degrees, though this was not as a result of a clever management strategy to play sites off against each other. It was rather that sites were still dependant upon regional market conditions and national laws, in this, a uniform development of individual sites at home or abroad was not feasible.

In many instances, the EWC was not integrated into negotiations by the management because it was considered as having no real importance, neither in respect to its institutional function nor to its behaviour. For example, the EWC was informed very late about the fact that the Belgian and Dutch sites were sold; the relevant interest-representing bodies at each site concerned were informed much earlier. Only the future will show if the protests by the EWC that followed- referring to the consequences on the basis of the court judgement in the Renault Vilvoorde case - will be able to change this approach.

Conclusion: The EWC - searching and isolated

The European level of representation currently only plays a minor role at the Kaefer company. All of the crucial developments with regard to the company are discussed with the national company or workplace. Problems are negotiated and - in most cases - solved by mutual agreement. With this in mind, it is not surprising that the EWC has major difficulties in defining its own role.

This special frame-work of bodies and institutions corresponds to the company structure and the relations between individual sites abroad and in the home country. The individual sites are only integrated to a small extent into the company's internal division of labour as they work almost exclusively within the regional markets. At the Kaefer company, employees would only very rarely work on orders relating to another site and geographic region.

This special nature of the construction industry means that competition for a certain location is limited only to the country itself. Another result of this special condition is the fact that the central company management scarcely exerts its overview authority, leaving the individual sites relatively autonomous - despite the new company structure - as long as the sites turn out the profit expected of them.

In our opinion, the constellation of the EWC within the relational structure of national worker representation, the management, and the trade unions can be characterised by the term "isolated EWC". It is true the EWC is actually an accepted institution that develops independent activities. But when seen within the context of re-structuring, the EWC finds itself in an isolated position (between the national representative bodies and the management) because site-specific aspects have much more importance than pan-European aspects or perspectives. This is the direct result of the company structure described above.

At the same time, this isolated position makes it necessary for the EWC to draw up an overview of its activity in the future developments. To a certain extent, the EWC can be characterised as searching a role for the future.

Case Study 5:[28] The European Works Council of AstraZeneca within the changing structure of the company

Concept and aim of the case study

The focus of interest of this case study is the rapid and fundamental change at the British pharmaceutical and chemical company Zeneca (today: AstraZeneca) which merged with the Swedish Astra company over a 13-month period. At the same time, the company pulled out of business areas that were previously considered very important, and planned further re-

---

[28] This case study was produced by Lionel Fulton and edited for this report.

structuring measures in order to transform itself into a company producing exclusively pharmaceutical products.

The main topic of this case study is the situation and function of the already existing European Works Council in the process of the changes. Of particular interest is the extent to which the EWC was informed about the company's plans before implementation, and how it was then able to affect or influence decisions.

The empirical survey uses information published by the company; the minutes of several EWC meetings; interviews with EWC members, trade unionists and the management of Zeneca.

The Zeneca Company

From the foundation of Zeneca to the year 1998 Zeneca was the result of the breakup of the British chemical giant ICI in 1993, when products such as pharmaceuticals, agrochemicals and special chemicals that require a high degree of research were combined in a new company called Zeneca. The split, announced in February 1993 and implemented in June of the same year, was justified in terms of the increasing competition within the world-wide market for chemicals and pharmaceutical products. It led to a reduction in the workforce from 114,000 to 109,000. The majority of jobs were lost at those units that could be considered the "ICI remainders". At the newly founded company Zeneca, approx. 2,000 workers had to be laid off.

Until recently, the three business areas (pharmaceutical products, agrochemicals and speciality chemicals) were the main elements of Zeneca's product range with a special focus on pharmaceutical products - with major profits in this area. Pharmaceuticals accounted only for one half of the total turnover.

Zeneca, as created, was a world-wide conglomerate with production sites in Europe, America, and Asia; although the UK remained the main focus of the company.

The distribution of the workforce is further proof of the former importance of the British part of the conglomerate. At the end of 1998, 40% of the total workforce of 34,600 (14,000) were employed in the UK, 33% in North and South America, 19% in the rest of Europe, and approx. 8% in Asia, Africa, and Australia. The key centres of employment of around 6,600 workers in Europe outside the UK were France, Germany, Italy, Spain, Belgium and the Netherlands, although Zeneca has workers in all EU countries except for Luxembourg.

Until 1998, there were no major changes to the conglomerate's strategy and no signs of any radical changes were apparent to anybody outside the company. Sir Sydney Lipworth, CEO of Zeneca said in his speech at the

Annual General Meeting on 25th of May, 1998 that the company had made decisive 'steps towards the declared goal of achieving the leading position in selected business areas'. He praised the results of all three business areas.

The only signs of a possible change could not be observed from within Zeneca, they were only visible from outside. For example, the CEO of Astra, Mr. Hakan Mogren, mentioned Zeneca as a potential partner in terms of the continuing consolidation of the pharmaceutical industry (Financial Times, June 8th, 1998) and indeed, the first meetings and talks had taken place between Astra and Zeneca in 1996.

Rapid developments 1999–1999 This relatively stable situation came to an end in November 1998, when Zeneca announced world-wide plans to sell the speciality chemicals business with around 5,500 employees. The decision was justified by the statement that speciality chemicals would have improved opportunities of growth when outside of the Zeneca company, especially because - according to Jeremy Scudamore (managing director of Zeneca Specialities) - the entire sector of speciality chemicals was undergoing a phase of 'rapid consolidation'.

Another reason for selling the speciality chemicals area - so it was said - was that it would 'increase the company's focussing on Zeneca Pharmaceuticals and Zeneca Agrochemicals' (Sir David Barnes, managing director of Zeneca plc - press statement from November 12, 1998).

This surprising news in November 1998 was topped by another, even bigger surprise only one month later when Zeneca announced a planned merger with the Swedish Astra company on December 9th that year.

The two companies had comparable turnover (Zeneca - £ 5.2 billion in 1997 and Astra - £ 4.3 billion). Both companies were third world-wide in the area of prescription drugs. The same ranking - according to the companies - applied to their expenditures for R&D. The new company was to be owned 53.5% by former Zeneca shareholders and 46.5% by former Astra shareholders.

Of the world-wide workforce of 55,000 employees (35,000 Zeneca and 20,000 Astra), around 6,000 were to be made redundant as part of a cost reduction program over a 3-year period.

Astra only invested in pharmaceutical products which clearly dominated the area of agrochemical products within the merged conglomerate. Despite this fact, the company claimed that 'The merger does not directly impact this business [agrochemicals]'.

The Zeneca management justified the merger in terms of the growth opportunities it would create and with the fact that the two companies were now provided with a complementary product portfolio. Tom McKillopp, managing director of pharmaceuticals for Zeneca said:

> Astra and Zeneca are a perfect match for each other... a similar management philosophy as well as a strongly scientific-based corporate identity make the companies natural partners. AstraZeneca has a strong potential for a profitable growth led by innovation.

The potential cost reductions resulting from the merger of the two conglomerates were not expressly stated, but the management expected cost reductions in the range of US$1.1 billion within a 3-year period.

The fast consolidation of the pharmaceutical industry was not mentioned in the official statement, but was surely a decisive factor in favour of the merger. During the weeks before the announcement of the Zeneca-Astra merger it was reported that the German concern Hoechst was going to merge with Rhône Poulenc and that Sanofi was going to merge with Synthélabo.

The merger of Zeneca and Astra was progressing very rapidly. After the merger was approved by the Offices for the Control and Supervision of Cartels in the EU and the USA and after being approved by the majority of the shareholders, the new company AstraZeneca was founded on April 6th, 1999.

Merger documentation made it clear that the planned sale of Speciality Chemicals was being followed up and on June 30th, 1999 it was finally sold.

This was not the end of the re-structuring measures at Zeneca (now AstraZeneca). On May 27th, 1999 the Financial Times reported that the company had decided to dispose of its agrochemicals as well.

The Financial Times cited low profits within agrochemicals as well as the cyclical nature of the business as the main reasons for this decision. In addition - according to the Financial Times - it would have been necessary to invest further in the company in order to maintain a competitive edge over rivals such as Monsanto.

The management would not confirm the report in the Financial Times. However, as early as August 1999, the management announced in the six-monthly business report a programme aiming at improving profits and guaranteeing the competitiveness of the agrochemical business. The programme was initiated in response to a difficult market situation. Only a short time later, the reduction of approx. 450 out of the 8,500 jobs in the division (Zeneca Agrochemicals) was announced and on October 28th, 1999, Tom McKillopp said that he would not rule out any option with regard to the business area's future.

On December 2nd 1999, AstraZeneca announced that Zeneca Agrochemicals was to be merged with the corresponding division of the Swiss company Novartis (Novartis Agribusiness) to form the new company Syngenta AG. The new company was to be founded in the second half of the year 2000. As a result of this merger, another 3,000 jobs were to be cut back world-wide.

It would be a mistake to assume that the process of change is complete - the contrary is probably to be expected. The developments described above occurred over only a few months and give a clear impression of the speed of the re-structuring measures faced by the workforce's representation.

Development, structure and problems of the EWC - the history of the EWC

The Zeneca European Works Council (today: AstraZeneca) has been active since the end of 1995. The voluntary agreement (in accordance with art. 13 of the Directive) was one of the first British EWC agreements to be signed, though talks and negotiations leading up to it date back to the end of the 1990s when Zeneca was still a part of ICI. The real engine of this process was the then national secretary for chemicals of the Transport and General Workers Union, who supported the introduction of the EWC together with the relevant Euro-federation (today EMCEF).

There were two meetings organised by the Transport and General Workers Union within the frame of the EU Household Directive 4004. The first meeting was held without the participation of the management, and rejected the general idea of an EWC. During the second meeting, the management invited the participants for dinner.

As a result of the split from ICI, the first steps were not followed-up. When negotiations were taken up again after some time, they seemed to be going quite well, as the new company wanted to distinguish itself from ICI. The draft of an EWC agreement was published in April 1995, leading to a pilot meeting after the announcement of the Zeneca interim report in September 1995. The big difference, when compared to the April draft, was the fact that the trade unions clearly played a more important role in the final draft.

The agreement The contents of the Zeneca agreement were considered rather typical for a UK company. The EWC, the Zeneca European Information and Consultation Committee, combined representatives of employers and employees are members. The board of the EWC was - more or less - the managing board (principally, the CEO of Zeneca was the chairman). All of the western European countries in which Zeneca operated were allowed to send their representatives.

The main task of the EWC was to discuss the 'company results, company developments, investment plans, and other affairs of major importance'. The EWC was seen as an instrument for 'informing and consulting the workforce on the European level'.

The company management did not expressly state that the EWC was going to be informed when major decisions were to be taken. The agreement itself states that Zeneca commits itself to 'the exchange of views with representatives of the workforce as well as to informing and consulting' not only with regard to 'the business developments of the company' but with regard to 'major changes that would concern two or more European countries'. An annex lists some examples with regard to the topics in this context:

- Company mergers, company acquisitions or company sales processes;
- major staff reductions, i.e. reductions concerning at least 50 employees in at least two or more European countries of one business area;
- major changes of the financial position of the company which affect the workforce.

The EWC of Zeneca consists of a total of 33 representatives of the company's employees; each Western European country with a company site sends at least one representative. The countries with a workforce of above 500 employees can send up to three representatives, Great Britain may send six. In total, the EWC was composed as indicated in the table below.

Table 5.2 Zeneca's EWC representatives

Country	Number of Representatives
Austria	1
Belgium	3
Denmark	1
Finland	1
France	3
Germany	3
Greece	1
Ireland	1
Italy	3
Norway	1
Portugal	1
Spain	3
Sweden	1
Switzerland	1
The Netherlands	3
U.K.	6
Total	33

The selection of representatives was mainly dependent upon the regulations and traditions of the laws and custom in each country. In the U.K., the six representatives of the "Central Business and General Committee" were the six members of the committee at the top of Zeneca's national system of information and consultation. (In contrast to most British companies and due to its ICI past, Zeneca is equipped with a well developed system of national information and consultation, consisting of committees at plant, sector and company level.)

The role of the trade unions was expressly emphasised in the agreement. According to the wishes of the workforce's representatives, up to six full-time trade union officers were empowered to participate in the preparatory meetings of the workforce, and three (two of them coming from the UK) were even allowed to participate in the general conference.

Zeneca's EWC had a committee to prepare the agenda; this was a kind of steering committee consisting of eight representatives (two from the UK) and was to meet about two months before the General Conference.

According to the agreement, there was to be one meeting "after the publication of the business results for the financial year and after the general meeting". Extraordinary meetings were not expressively mentioned in the text of the agreement; but in the annex, you can find the paragraph below that allows extraordinary meetings:

> In addition to the regular exchange of information, evaluations, and opinions it is considered useful in the case of major changes to enter into a process of consultation and dialogue when Zeneca as a whole or employees of one or two European countries are concerned. The company is obliged - as far as possible - to guarantee an open dialogue and an open exchange of opinions between the members of the European Information and Consultation Committee and central management.

The agreement also defines how discussions within the EWC are to be reported to the workforces of the individual countries and companies: One summary will be supplied by the management in English. This summary is distributed and can then be translated if the need arises on site.

As with most British EWC agreements, confidentiality is an important factor within the document. The annex states that EWC members are not allowed to pass confidential information to third parties. At the same time, management reserves the right to withhold information from the EWC if the information concerned:

is objectively and in accordance with the account rendering regulations of a kind that is suited to considerably disturb or precedent the development of business processes.

External experts are not mentioned in the agreement although trade union officers who were listed in this category in other EWC agreements are given the right to participate in the meetings.

As usual, travel expenses are borne by the company. The management is responsible for organising the meeting and for translations required; it also provides the secretariat.

The EWC's work during the first three years

Until 1998, the EWC operated without major problems. In accordance with the agreement, meetings were held once a year in Spring in order to inform about or discuss current problems. The events of the meeting in 1998 as below give a good example:

- Sir David Barnes, the company's CEO made the opening speech; he roughly sketched the strategic developments of the last financial year and described future goals.
- The chairman of the employee's representatives (from the U.K.) and the deputy chairman of the employee's representatives (from Germany) answered and informed the meeting about the key topics and requests of the employees.
- Information about global financial events of the past year.
- Some detailed questions were directed at the company's CEO that resulted in further discussion and that were mostly answered by the management representatives.
- There was a discussion on Health and Safety at Work as well as environmental topics.
- Additional points on the agenda with regard to the work of the EWC.
- There was an introduction to an important general topic of Zeneca. On this occasion, the effects of the Single European Currency (EURO) were discussed.

The Belgian representative raised an interesting question with regard to harmonisation and asked if the share option that the British would profit from could be made accessible to the other national workforces as well. The management promised to look into the possibilities.

In the first few years following the agreement there were only minor changes in the composition of EWC; e.g. when the Belgian representation was reduced from three to two due to changes in the company.

All in all, the work of the EWC during the first three years seemed to be quite successful for the majority of the participants. A British employee representative said that not only had he gained a better understanding of the company's activity as a whole, but that the workforce's representatives could really influence management. A German and an Italian representative praised the efficient work of the EWC and Sir David Barnes, the then Zeneca CEO, said that the opportunity afforded to the EWC to discuss matters on an European level was very valuable indeed for management and the workforce.

The EWC's work since 1998

The Zeneca decision to sell off the Speciality Chemicals division hit the normal routine of the EWC like a bombshell. Although the agreement did not expressly mention extraordinary meetings, one was instantly convened in order to discuss the separation: The decision was announced on November 12th and the extraordinary meeting was held on November 17th 1998.

The CEO of Zeneca, Sir David Barnes, admitted to the fact that the news was a bit of a shock, especially for those people who worked in this business area. The decision had been taken at the board meeting in October of 1998 after it had become obvious that a process of consolidation had started in the area of Speciality Chemicals.

The board was convinced that, mindful of the specialist nature of the business area, its successful future could only lie with a company larger than Zeneca.

Sir David Barnes underlined the fact that announcing the plans at this point in time indicated clearly the openness of their management style. They could have waited until a buyer was found with the result that there would have been no consultation at all.

The workforce representatives did not hide the fact that they were surprised by the news, particularly because management had repeatedly assured the EWC that the future of Speciality Chemicals was within Zeneca. One emphasised the fact that questions had been asked with regard to the future of this business area in previous meetings, but that the management had never indicated or even hinted at the possible sale of the unit. After this latest development, it was doubtful whether the credibility of the management could still be deemed intact.

Despite this kind of harsh criticism (which was shared by most of the employee's representatives) the workforce representative put forward several substantial demands. Firstly, the management should continuously inform and consult with regard to the sales process. Secondly, the employee representatives expressed their strong wish to sell the business area as an entity to a buyer who was able to offer the employees concerned a long-term working future. Thirdly, the workforce demanded that no personal disadvantages should arise for the workers concerned.

Management ignored the proposal of one of the German representatives to create a "communication network" with the power to negotiate and which would deal with any information in confidence. The representatives were referred to the local consulting instances that were responsible for such affairs. (It must be doubtful anyway that such a demand would have been supported by all of the workforce's representatives. The British trade union TGWU would certainly have had a problem with it.)

During the second, even larger re-structuring - the merger with Astra - the EWC members seemed to be taken by surprise as much as the first time. This was due to the developments within the pharmaceutical industry described above. An extraordinary meeting of the EWC was summoned on December 14th, 1998, shortly after the merger was announced on December 8th. The employee representatives did not miss the opportunity to emphasise the contrast between the merger decision and statements at the regular EWC conference of the previous year when the management said that there was no reason at all for seeking a merger and hinted at risks of creating too large a conglomerate.

The employee representatives complained that nothing had been said at the extraordinary EWC meeting a month before when the management must have known about the possibility of a merger, and they criticised this lack of trust and openness.

The way the merger was announced was heavily criticised with the workforce's representatives only becoming aware of the merger via newspapers and TV. Sir David Barnes' statement that the news was released earlier than originally planned as detail about the merger had been leaked to the media failed to assure the annoyance of the EWC members. One of the EWC members said he thought that trust in the openness and values of Zeneca had certainly suffered as a result of current events.

During the debate that followed, the planned cut in jobs was the main topic. The EWC wanted to know if it was necessary to cut 6,000 jobs; one wanted to know how the loss of employment was distributed between Zeneca and Astra - not only on a global scale, but also with regard to individual countries - and if the reduction in the workforce could not be avoided. The management's response to most questions of this kind stated that it was much too early to give an answer at all although hopes were high that the reduction of workplaces could be achieved on a voluntary basis.

The possible participation of the EWC in the negotiations on the framework of conditions for the cut in workforce was not discussed.

Other topics discussed were the process of harmonising wages and working conditions between Astra and Zeneca in the individual countries, the future of the Agrochemicals division within the new conglomerate, and the necessity for a re-formed EWC after the merger.

The management stated that it was too early in time to give detailed answers to most of the questions posed. It was emphasised though that a new EWC was to be set up for the new company and that the Agrochemicals division would not be touched by the merger - at least not directly. Of course, re-structuring within the agrochemicals industry was a necessary fact and moreover Zeneca would have to monitor the developing situation closely in order to be able to take the necessary steps to maintain the division's competitive edge.

On May 10th, 1999, the EWC steering committees of Zeneca and Astra met in order to consult on a constitution for the new, joint EWC. After ascertaining that no major differences existed between both agreements they compromised on a new text that was largely based on the existing Zeneca agreement. Prior to that, the management had already proposed to use the Zeneca agreement as a model.

The major deviations from the Zeneca agreement in the final draft were in the composition of committee that now integrated the countries of Central and Eastern Europe and, at the same time, reducing the number of representatives per country. The two remaining business areas (Agrochemicals and Pharmaceuticals) were treated separately, leading to a slight overrating of the British compared to the Swedish input. Other modifications were the reference to express the possibility of inviting external experts and to expand the steering committee to eight members. The composition is now as shown on Table 5.3.

Table 5.3 Composition of the EWC AstraZeneca

Country	Number of Representatives	Number of Employees
Austria	1	179
Belgium	2	739
Czech Republic	1	162
Denmark	1	261
Finland	1	153
France	3	2011
Germany	3	1981
Greece	2	247
Hungary	1	184
Ireland	1	72
Italy	3	1759
Norway	1	172
Poland	1	202
Portugal	1	220
Spain	2	889
Sweden	4	8138
Switzerland	1	153
The Netherlands	2	386
U.K.	7	12648
Total	33	30556

On June 16th and 17th, 1999 all of the EWC representatives of both companies met for the first time. The items on the agenda were: A report from the CEO of the conglomerate, Tom McKillop, with regard to the integration of the companies, the signing of the proposed new agreement of the joint EWC, the latest developments in the sales process of the Speciality Chemicals division, and health and safety at work within the company as well as its environmental policy.

The proposed agreement was accepted with the exception of a few aspects that were to be clarified by the steering committees. In addition, there was a lengthy discussion on health and safety topics in order to create a list of focal points.

The last EWC meeting of this 13-month period of extraordinary events at Zeneca resp. AstraZeneca (a period starting in November of 1998) was held in December 1999, when an extraordinary meeting of the joint EWC was convened in order to discuss the planned merger of the Agrochemical business of AstraZeneca with the agro-business of Novartis.

This time, the EWC was called together on the same day that the merger was announced. Invitations were distributed the evening before. The stock exchanges were informed at 7.30 a.m., the EWC meeting started at 10.00 a.m., and the full-time trade union officers were informed at 8.30 a.m.

There were no major surprises during this meeting. The developments concerning the splitting of the conglomerate could not be ignored, although the management did not formally confirm it and the name of the merging partner was not known beforehand. Again, the loss of workplaces and the planning of the merger formed the centre of discussion.

The assessment by the participants

As mentioned above, Zeneca Great Britain held a well developed national system of information and consultation dating back to the ICI past of the company. This system supplied well functioning lines between committees on three levels - employees, business divisions (Speciality Chemicals, Agrochemicals, and Pharmaceuticals), and on company level. This fact, (that is to be considered as an exception for a British employer) explains why the British workforce representatives of Zeneca cannot understand that the EWC is to be considered as a new source of information. Some of them expressed fears that the management could attempt to undermine national structures through the EWC, resulting in major disadvantages as the EWC would not be integrated into the entire structure.

These fears were not entirely unfounded. The management had already admitted that - from its point of view - the national structures were too clumsy and needed renewing (this statement was made before outsourcing the Agrochemicals division). The situation is simplified by the separation of this business area, because now one level is eliminated. The establishment of the EWC allowed for international relations between the workforce representatives but it was unfortunate that the connections were mostly kept to the level of the steering committee, particularly because the differences between the divisions were proving to be simply too big. It would have been a good idea to establish connections and links between representatives of the same business areas within individual countries but this did not happen.

Finally, the company's re-structuring measures (about which the EWC was not informed, until after they had been decided) have certainly damaged the trust and confidence of the representatives towards the real value of the committee.

From the management's perspective, the EWC was designed as a committee where the leading representatives of the workforce could learn about the conglomerate's strategy directly from the management. The

German and Dutch representatives demanded a committee that would meet more often, perhaps even four times a year, engaging in practical work. This proposal was rejected by the group's management. Moreover, the most important achievement of the discussion was the focus on strategy.

At the beginning, discussions started hesitantly because everything was so new and the cultural differences were obvious. But now, discussions are much more lively and always focus on the core issue, for example, the conglomerate's CEO had to answer questions from the EWC regarding the purpose of the merger with Astra for three hours during an extraordinary meeting.

The management emphasised that proper consultation over the results of the decision would still take place at local/plant level and that as a company, management generally tried to avoid any surprises for the workforce, however, reproaches were justified when selling the business area of Speciality Chemicals was announced. This was obviously a great shock to many employees, who believed that the management did not comply with the promised consultation procedure. Afterwards, the management acknowledged that they had missed the opportunity to indicate the possibility of the sale much more clearly beforehand.

At AstraZeneca and the former Zeneca there are only a few areas - according to the management representative - where a company-wide policy exists; for example: health and safety at work, the environment, pension schemes for people working abroad, and general human resources management. All these policies are only sketched out in general and apply not only to Europe, but globally. To a certain extent, the EWC would not be able to exert any influence on these policies.

The full-time British trade union officer responsible for Zeneca, who regularly attended the EWC meetings, was also of the opinion that the sale of Speciality Chemicals was the reason for serious problems which resulted in a breakdown in the trust between the parties concerned.

He did not mean that the EWC should play a more important role in negotiations following such decisions. It would be wrong for EWC to be involved in negotiating staff cuts, and still worse, if it should be seen to interfere with collective bargaining. Such matters were to remain the responsibility of the trade unions. As a trade unionist, he would not be prepared to discuss such topics with the management, if any non-trade unionists sat at the table.

According to him, the EWC should deal with topics such as the environment, a minimum level of old age pension, or with equal opportunities. These were areas where success would be achievable and maybe one could also try to have such discussions co-ordinated by the Euro-federation.

Conclusion: The EWC - overwhelmed

It has become clear that the EWC had never been informed beforehand about major changes at Zeneca and AstraZeneca respectively, and that it was not able to exert any influence on the process of change.

The reason for this lies in the management's information policy. Obviously, management was not prepared to pass on vital information in time but believed it sufficient to explain the reasons leading to the decision later. The extensive questioning after the announcement of the merger with Astra proves this, and management has learned from experience, as the extraordinary meeting of the EWC proves, convened on the very day when management announced the latest re-structuring measure, the sale of the Agrochemicals business.

However, EWC members still depend on the media or vague statements from the management for more detailed information about important decisions and details of the conglomerate's development. A British representative reported that one could easily get just as much information about the merger plans with Novartis from the Internet as was given at the meeting by the management itself.

The reason behind the fact that the EWC is without any real influence lies both in the management and interest representation. The management was never really keen to consult the EWC about the consequences of its decisions. As the management states: Consultation will take place at the local/plant level.

The attitude of the employee representatives was different. While some, like the Germans, were interested, the majority, including the leading British trade unions, were not of the opinion that this kind of discussion was a central topic of the EWC. This was also the position of the influential British full-time trade union officer from the TGWU.

With this in mind, it is understandable that no pressure was exerted in order to give the EWC a leading role in discussions.

So, what tasks remain for the EWC? According to the management, there are only a few areas within the conglomerate that should be reconsidered at a European level. The possibilities for EWC participation are therefore rather small if it accepts this view. Still, there are signs that the EWC - after a slow start - has begun to consult and to try to exert an influence on questions such as health and safety, the environment, and share options for the workforce.

It also turned out that the major changes of the last 13 months occurred so suddenly that the EWC did not have an opportunity to develop an independent approach. Rather, the EWC has had to deal in its practical work with the consequences of these decisions, related to the future shape of the EWC.

There is not enough information to draw clear conclusions about the relations between the individual EWC members. It seems, though, that there are closer contacts, especially within the steering committee, even though this work has been made more difficult by the re-structuring measures.

It remains to be seen how far the EWC will be able to strengthen its position in the future. This would require a period of calm and an end of the re-structuring. With the ongoing consolidation process of the pharmaceutical industry in mind, it would be risky to assume this would happen.

Cornerstones of the linking of national and European levels of employee representation

Overall, the case studies reveal differing relations between the national and European levels of employee representation.

Given some of the major differences it is our opinion that there are several basic requirements for linking national and European levels.[29]

- A prerequisite of an efficient EWC is a clear understanding among its members of their function and the need to develop an independent role for the EWC.
- Furthermore, the EWC needs to be accepted by those individuals, i.e. the national employee representatives, the trade unions, and the company's management.
- The national representatives will have to integrate the European level into the way they operate and deal with partners at plant and company level.
- In addition, all experience and empirical surveys have shown that employee representatives have to build up an informal information and communication network in order to be able to develop successful activity. This applies especially to information and communication in between the EWC meetings.
- Finally, the intensive integration of full-time trade union officers into the dialogue with management as well as into the EWC itself is

---

[29] Compare the considerations in European Metalworkers' Federation / Centre for Strategic Trade Union Management: Cranfield University: European Works Councils in re-structuring situations; Discussion Paper 9, September 1999.

of major importance if we are to see an active role for the EWC. There has to be a successful combination of powers, both of national organisations and those representing European interests.

6. Future prospects - Developing industrial relations in Europe as a contradictory process between national and European regulation

The following conclusion refers to the interviews we had with trade unionists and management representatives from the four countries and at the European level as well as to the company case studies. Relevant literature has also been quoted. The conclusion is a mixture of the "classical" conclusion of a research study and a list of possible outcome of action that would be found in an "Executive Summary". The results are presented as theses that represent a selection of the major results of our study. They are no substitute for reading the report in detail, but they help to put the issues into perspective.

Thesis 1: Europeanisation as a multi-Level regulation

During the past years, a multi-level system of state regulation has been formed in Europe. In future it seems unlikely that there will be a return to the encompassing responsibility of the national state or the dissolution into a new European Federal State.

The development of industrial relations in Europe as one of the major aspects of the social dimension of European integration does not involve a standardisation of systems across Europe. In view of the complexity of the conditional factors of industrial relations in the individual countries, as well as characterising the integration process as a multi-level regulation, it is not possible to develop a concept of the Europeanisation of industrial relations that can be reduced only to the question of an increasing convergence of the systems. Europeanisation can be understood as a complex process of:

- the reorganisation of the levels of regulation, and
- the functional change and the modifications of the sub-systems at European, national, regional and company level.

Thesis 2: Trade unions as co-designers of this open Europeanisation process

With regard to this thesis, it should be noted that the reorganisation of industrial relations represents at the same time a reaction to the challenges of the globalisation of the economy and the implementation of new production (focussing on plant level, new forms of work organisations, etc.). Moreover, it must be said that the further development of industrial relations in Europe does not follow any objective logic, but is advancing its aims by means of arguments and conflicts on social issues. At a first glance the trade union response is contradictory in demanding and implementing a European-level regulation as well as in trying to keep the national status quo. A detailed view reveals that this is not a strategic fault because trade unions simply cannot ask in the abstract for the best possible level of regulation for the single aspects of industrial relations, but must consider the predominant relations of power and the existing framework. To clarify this point: the trade union approach is not an ideal and well-acknowledged strategy for tackling new tasks, but involves adapting to reality that displays many deficits and that originated from the lack of time and the lack of comprehensive prospects for the future. The problem is that the weaknesses will not be overcome by the supposed contradiction between keeping the national status quo and an expansion of European regulation.

Thesis 3: The European Works Councils as a future core element of Europeanisation?

In the present context, only EWCs show some potential within Europe on regulations for influencing industrial relations.

In all four countries covered by our research, employers' associations do not attach far-reaching strategic importance to EWCs. In particular, EWCs are not considered the core of the Europeanisation of industrial relations - in the sense of an expansion of the regulation competence on the European level. They are either considered superfluous or their importance is simply seen in terms of information exchange and a way of integrating employees into the company's strategy.

In contrast, the trade unions see it quite differently: Generally, EWCs are considered to be the major tool for strengthening cross-border trade union co-operation within the Euro-company. Of course, there are major differences in opinion between the individual countries on what the strengthening of the cross-border co-operation within the frame of the EWC should look like. At the same time, the political perspective of the EWC is not limited to the corresponding company. It is considered as a major starting point to extend the European level of industrial relations fully in every day life of trade unions. The future of the role of the EWC in concrete terms is in dispute. Until now, the trade unions have almost exclusively dealt with the establishment of EWCs in as many companies as possible. All those interviewed agreed that the EWC should undergo a slight but still significant revaluation. As far as works agreements are concerned, which are already the daily collective bargaining practice of national systems, even the possibility of signing work agreements by the EWC was rather welcomed.

Our conclusions assume that the EWC has only a relatively limited independent authority. The EWC therefore only develops an efficient political practice if it is broadly accepted by those individuals with access to sufficient information, and at the same time, has a concept of its own activities. This includes in particular developing an independent view of the EWC, overcoming the internal and external communication and information problems, and developing a strategy that will inform its practical work. Of utmost importance is effective co-operation with the individual representatives from each country. The EWC's capabilities should not be overrated. EWCs were initiated as the new response to the increasing internationalisation of company structures as the national bodies at plant and company level could no longer deal with this. Hitherto, the EWC has only been able to compensate to a small degree the losses of possibilities for action nationally.

Thesis 4: Repercussions of Europeanisation on national industrial relations

Seeing EWCs to be an element of a future Europeanisation of industrial relations, those interviewed could not - not least due to the relatively short time of each EWC - identify any repercussions of the EWC's work on national industrial relations on the basis of their own empirical experience. In addition, it has to be acknowledged that the EWC Directive was implemented nationally, i.e. adapted according to the conditions and regulations of the existing national systems of industrial relations.

For example, German trade unionists have hinted at the company-level union agreement tendencies that developed independently from the existence of the EWC. This development increases in importance in combination with another trend observed by the interviewees: Increasingly, major industrial companies in the chemical industry, and also the food industry, are attempting to standardise their human resource management across Europe, or at least they try to achieve a better co-ordination in Europe. This leads to an interest employees and the trade unions have in a stronger European standardisation of the bodies representing their interests. Vice versa, management as well may develop an interest to have a partner on the European level who would take responsibility where controversial questions have to be settled. Within such a framework and in the medium term, EWCs could become more important and could modify the German works constitution. The signing of works agreements as part of general collective bargaining could be a result of the developments at hand, particularly so as works agreements are the rule in many EU countries. In other countries, most of all in the U.K., the fear of a Euro-syndicalism is interpreted as typically German, as here - different from Germany - the plant/company level is the decisive field for collective bargaining.

The employer representatives did not observe any repercussions on national industrial relations. They emphasised the fact that they did not have empirical data on the work of EWCs. In the UK, some employer representatives even acknowledged the need to reconsider the national representative structures.

The following conclusions can be drawn from the case studies in terms of the impacts on the national systems of representation:

- A prerequisite of an effective EWC is a clear understanding among its members of their function and the development of an independent identity of the EWC.
- The EWC needs to be accepted by those involved, i.e. the national representatives, the trade unions, and the management.
- The national representative bodies have to take account of European level activities as well as their workplace or company activities.
- Experience and empirical surveys have clearly shown that representative organisations at national and European level must build formal and informal networks of information and communication to develop successful activities. This especially

includes information and communication in between the official EWC meetings.
- Finally, the active involvement of full-time trade union officers and dialogue with management as well as within the EWC are of major importance to create an active role for the EWC, and ensure the successful co-operation of national and European representatives.

Thesis 5: "Europeanisation" of collective bargaining policy within multi-level regulation

Currently, within the collective bargaining policy, it is not possible to detect an attempt at forming a European level of regulation. Now, as before, collective bargaining policy is formulated on a national level and determined by a balance of power there. On the one hand, this is based upon the fact that employers reject any negotiations on a European level resp. refuse to create corresponding associative structures. On the other hand, even trade unions show some scepticism about negotiations on the European level. Among other things, the question of how far the trade unions consider themselves powerful enough to win through outside the national framework (e.g. in view of the lack of a European right to strike) is responsible for this fact.

Meanwhile, there is a "makeshift" policy on Europe-wide co-ordinated collective bargaining, (covering the Euro regions as well as the adaptation of working hours regulations) in order to avoid wage dumping resp. in order to limit the corresponding disadvantages despite all differences in system, level, and interest.

However, given the current conditions, this will only be the start of a proactive collective bargaining policy at European level. In general there is not yet any co-ordination between trade unions of individual countries in the strict sense of the word with any strategic goals.

Consequently and with regard to collective bargaining, the legislator should play an increasingly important role at European level (catchword: Social Dialogue?), however he only partly fulfils this requirement. There is a second area of collective bargaining available at company level where the EWC would have to accept an important role. If only the EWC would be able to live up to the task respectively, it should accept the job from the trade union point of view, only time can tell.

When attempting to assess the extent of Europeanisation of collective bargaining one must differentiate between the five levels of Europeanisation of wage policy (arranged in order of the degree of coordination):

- Information between the trade unions of the countries.
- Co-operation.
- Co-ordination between national trade unions and Euro-federations.
- Handing over of responsibilities to Euro-federations.
- Merging of the national (industries) trade unions into one Euro-federation.

The current development is located somewhere between the first and the second level.

Thesis 6: The Social Dialogue as a "European Supplement" to national collective bargaining

In our opinion, Social Dialogue is no replacement for free collective bargaining; on the other hand, it is a necessary supplement in addition to national systems of industrial relations, it is a "European supplement", so to speak. Strengthening those involved at European level would be a condition for any further expansion of the Social Dialogue - this is, due to different reasons, not (yet) within reach. Moreover, other important questions remain to be clarified, e.g. the question of the legality of the agreement; questions that possibly will have to be solved within a collective bargaining framework. Another open and much disputed question is the connection between the Social Dialogue and European Works Councils, i.e. the line between the level of the (legal) institution and the level of the actors: How could the EWC support the implementation of the Social Dialogue or would it be possible that European Works Councils - even within the framework of the "companising" that is being observed - receive design and contractual responsibilities within the frame of the Social Dialogue?

With regard to sector specific social Dialogue in accordance with the Social Protocol, the new process has had no consequences or effects - no skeleton agreements currently exist - with the exception of the transport industry. The employers are even less prepared than on the level of the general Social Dialogue to discuss guidelines with regard to common aspects with the trade unions and to submit them for signing by the EU Commission; UNICE does not even distinguish between individual sectors of industry yet.

This is the reason for the fact that some national trade unions consider the co-ordination of their collective bargaining policies as the only way out of the weakness which they particularly experience within the sectoral Social Dialogue (see above).

Thesis 7: Complex interweaving of National and European association structures

All in all, with regard to the employer organisations and the wide field of industrial relations, it can be said that sufficient association structures do not exist that would allow the conclusion of binding agreements. Firstly, this is not desired politically as the national associations and particularly the companies themselves insist on their autonomy. Secondly, this is due to the very heterogeneous structure of the existing associations. Thirdly, the single national employers' associations have very different functions, so that people in Europe have to agree on the smallest common denominator.

This means that trade unions in Europe depend upon guaranteeing a complex balance of interests between the national member associations if they want to develop an independent handling competence.

However, the relationship is not without tensions - with differences between the individual sectors - between national trade unions and their respective Euro-confederations (currently undergoing a massive process of change). In the mid-Eighties, the confederations were founded as EU lobbyists. Today, they are to be re-formed to become efficient organisations with Euro responsibilities (these are still plans for the future) that shall sort out the information flow between the national trade unions in a way that would make the (currently quite laborious) methods of bilateral information superfluous. This leads to massive changes in the structures of the Euro-federations and the tasks of those involved. The changes are developing along two lines:

1. Firstly, the sector of industry - independent of the countries - is a distinguishing criterion. Greater international co-operation is only developing where concrete trade union interests are observed, e.g. in the chemical industry and in the metal industry (cross-border regional co-operations).
2. Secondly, the individual framework conditions of the countries determine the development of the Euro-federations: This results in the fact that at least in the German and British trade unions, there is a gradual erosion in the opposition to Europeanisation. It is true that the level of national organisations still dominate, but a division of labour is developing slowly in a painful and contradictory way and connecting the two levels. Understanding and common sense make it obvious that it is only by combining both levels that one can increase one's own problem-solving competence. Currently, trade unions seem to be burdened with the task of implementing reforms in both the national and European contexts as existing structures and patterns of behaviour

are no longer sufficient for managing the manifold tasks. French and Italian trade unions are still very much nationally oriented. Despite the euphoric Euro-rhetoric one will have to wait for a fundamental change in practice.

Thesis 8: The modified role of the (European) legislature

Government intervention at a European level has a different character than on the national level. This fact is reflected in what happens in individual countries. In Germany and France European law is significantly more non-committal than the national state's law (as those two countries are highly regulated by law), while from the British point of view, there is a considerable increase in the level of state regulation.

There are "coalitions of attitudes" with regard to the role of the European legislature concerning the regulation of industrial relations between the two sides of industry along national state lines (e.g. in the UK between the trade unions and the employers' associations) and there are corresponding (cross-border) coalitions according to the "two sides of industry" model (meaning significant differences between trade unions and employer's associations) of attitude The different degree of regulation that forms the basis of these coalitions within the individual countries is a kind of matrix: for example while trade unions in Germany fear a deterioration of industrial relations by European legislation and the employers in Germany hope for a more flexible development of what they see as "too rigid" regulation in Germany by the European legislator, trade unions and employers in the U.K. are both interested in a degree of regulation of industrial relations - if for different reasons.

In terms of the actual "output" of European industrial relations legislation, it is remarkable that there is not greater standardisation. The laws on EWCs, the European company (SE) and the Social Dialogue are mainly procedures. There are only a few rights and duties which are specified for the two sides of the industry.

Thesis 9: Europeanisation of industrial relations as a designing moment within the globalisation process - a German future?

There is considerable pressure coming from globalisation (e.g. mergers by "global players", relocation of plants outside Europe, accelerated development of technology, and dramatic reductions of product development cycles, unhampered and uncontrolled capital flow) and the implementation of new production processes. This result is a move to representation at corporate level, undermining national regulation mechanisms by international company strategies. These trends are only being marginally slowed down by countermeasures at European level. Current institutions and procedures cannot prevent the undermining of structures and institutions - such as the comprehensive (national/regional) system of collective bargaining and co-determination at plant/company level. On the other hand, the expanding institutions involved in the Europeanisation of industrial relations - that develop on the basis of the multi-level regulation of thesis 1 - have an impact on a basic flexibility of the German system of industrial relations. This readiness in principle and ability to open the national system to other influences can indeed be used to give the German system more flexibility and make it "ready" to prepare itself (mentally) for globalisation processes without having to experience any dramatic break-downs.

Such a "strategy" would correspond to the century-old tradition of the German trade unions, who maintain that it is certainly better to interfere in the (political) process right from the beginning and thus to seize all opportunities for co-determination, rather than to organise resistance to inevitable developments.

Bibliography

Baglioni, G. (1998), Illustrazione e commento dell'accordo Luglio '97, in: *L'impresa al plurale. Quaderni della partecipazione*, No. 1, pp. 53-63.
Baumann, H., Laux, E.-L., Schnepf, M. (1997), *Tarifverhandlungen im europäischen Baugewerbe - europäische Tarifverhandlungen?, Schluß bericht des Projektes der FES Brüssel, der EFBH und der IG BAU*, Bruxelles.
Benz-Overhage, K. (1999), *Statement zur geplanten Richtlinie über eine europäische Aktiengesellschaft für eine Pressekonferenz am 15.4.1999.*
Blank, M., Geissler, S. and Jaeger, R. (1996), *Euro-Betriebsräte: Grundlagen, Praxisbeispiele, Mustervereinbarungen*, Köln.
Braun, S., Eberwein, W. and Tholen, J. (1992), *Belegschaften und Unteneh mer. Zur Geschichte und Soziologie der deutschen Betriebsverfassung und Belegschaftsmitbestimmung*, Frankfurt/M., New York.
Buatier, M. (1995), *Die Branche der Elektrohaushaltsgeräte*, IESS-AE, Rom 1995.
Burgess, P. (1997), Branchentarifverhandlungen in Europa: Flächentarif à la carte?, in: *WSI-Mitteilungen*, vol. 50, No. 2, pp. 112-18.
Buschak, W. (1998), *Die Umsetzung der EBR-Richtlinie in nationales Recht*, Europäischer Gewerkschaftsbund, Brüssel.
Buschak, W (1998), Konturen eines europäischen Mitbestimmungsrahmens, in: *Mitbestimmung*, vol. 44, no. 1 and 2, pp. 64-65.
Carrieri, M. (1996a), I consigli di sorveglianza: come si traducono nell' esperienza italiana, in: *Lavoro Informazione*, no. 13, pp. 5-13.
Carrieri, M. (1998), Zanussi: dal modello al sistema, in: *L'impresa al plural. Quaderni della partecipazione*, no. 1, pp. 95-102.
Castro, M. (1998), La rinnovata costituzione partecipativa di Electolux Zanussi: profumo di controriforma?, in: *L'impresa al plurale, Quaderni della partecipazione*, no. 1, pp. 65-93.
Cattero, B. (1999), Beteiligung, Partizipation, Mitbestimmung – das Statut der Europäischen Aktiengesellschaft und der babylonische Turm europäischer Arbeitsbeziehungen, in: *Zeitschrift für Rechtssoziologie* vol. 20, no. 2, pp. 262-82.
Danone, Dokumentation der IUL zur transnationalen Kooperation bei Danone, *Danone Bulletin 1*, November 1997 etc.
Deppe, J., Hoffmann, R. and Stützel, W. (eds.) (1997), *Europäische Betriebsräte - Wege in ein soziales Europa*, Frankfurt/M., New York.

Dörre, K. (1995), Postfordismus und industrielle Beziehungen - Die Gewerkschaften zwischen Standortkonkurrenz und ökologisch-sozialer Reformpolitik, in: E. Bulmahn, P. v. Oertzen and J. Schuster (eds.): *Jenseits von Öko-Steuern, Dortmund*, pp. 145-72.

Dörre, K. (1996), Globalstrategien von Unternehmen - Ein Desintegrations - phänomen, *SOFI-Mitteilungen* no. 24. pp. 15-27.

Dufour, Ch., Hege, A. and Rehfeldt, U. (1992), *Systemes de Representation des Salaries dans l' Établissements en Grande-Bretagne et en Italie, Rapport Final*, IRES, Paris.

Ebbinghaus, B., Visser, J. (1997), Der Wandel der Arbeitsbeziehungen im westeuropäischen Vergleich, in S. Hradil, S. Immerfall (eds.), *Die west europäischen Gesellschaften im Vergleich*, Opladen, pp. 333-76.

Eberwein, W. and Tholen, J. (1993), *Euro-Manager or Splendid Isolation? International Management - An Anglo-German Comparison*, Berlin, New York.

ETUC (1999), *Towards an European system of industrial relations. Specific resolution (draft). For the 9th congress of ETUC Helsinki July 1999*, Bruxelles.

Ferner A. and Hyman, R. (1993), *Industrial Relations in the New Europe*, Oxford.

Financial Times (1998), *Euro-Launch*, 15.-18.12.1998.

FIOM CGIL Piemonte/Osservatorio sulla contrattazione e sulle condizioni di lavoro (1997), *Sistemi di relazioni sindacali: Testo Unico Zanussi - Accordo Fiat 18 marzo 1996, a cura di Piero Pessa*, Torino.

Fürstenberg, F. (1958), Der Betriebsrat – Strukturanalyse einer Grenzinstitution, in: *Kölner Zeitschrift für Soziologie und Sozialpsychologie*, vol. 10, no. 3, pp. 418-429.

Geissler, S., Krieger, H. (1996): Europäische Betriebsräte: Aktivitäten der Europäischen Stiftung zur Verbesserung der Arbeits- und Lebensbedingungen, in: *WSI-Mitteilungen*, vol. 49, no. 8, pp. 527-28.

Gerstenberger-Sztana, B. (1996), Europäische Betriebsräte in der Metallindustrie - Praktische Erfahrungen des Europäischen Metallgewerkschaftsbundes, in: *WSI-Mitteilungen*, vol. 49, no. 8, pp. 513-19.

Gollbach, J. and Schulten, Th. (1999), Tarifpolitik unter dem Euro und der Bildungsbedarf bei tarifpolitischer Koordinierung in Tarifpartnerschaften, *Arbeit und Politik, Mitteilungsblätter der Akademie für Arbeit und Politik an der Universität Bremen*, no. 26, 1999, pp. 47-53.

Groupe Alpha/Ires-Cgil (1997), Cas n° 4: Electrolux – Plan mondial, Zanussi - accord Italien, *Groupa Alpha/Info-Institut/Ires-Cgil/Lasaire, Conditions d'efficacite pratique de la consultation des comites d'entreprise europeens en situation de restructuration*, vol. 2: Dossiers Monographiques, unpublished report.

Gruppo Electrolux-Zanussi (1997), *Testo Unico sul sistema di relazioni sindacali e di partecipazione. Gruppo Electrolux-Zanussi, 21 luglio 1997*.

Hege, A. and Dufour, Ch. (1995), Decentralization and Legitimacy in Employee Representation: A Franco-German Comparison, in: *European Journal of Industrial Relations*, vol. 1, no. 1, pp. 83-99.

Helbig, M. (1997), *Strukturkonvergenzen und Kommunikationsschwierig keiten als Kooperationshemmnisse in Europäischen Betriebsräten*, Diplomarbeit an der Ruhr-Universität Bochum, Fakultät Sozialwissenschaften.

Helfert, M. (1992), Betriebsverfassung, neue Rationalisierungsformen, lean production, in: *WSI-Mitteilungen*, vol. 45, no. 8, pp. 505-21.

Hemmer, E. (1998), Erfahrungsbericht über den Europäischen Betriebsrat im ARBED-Konzern, in: W. Eberwein and J. Tholen (eds.), *Euro-Betriebsräte und deutsche Betriebsverfassung*, pp. 44-54.

Höland, A. (1997), *Mitbestimmung und Europa, aus der Reihe "Mitbestimmung und neue Unternehmenskulturen"*, Bertelsmann-Stiftung und HBS, Gütersloh.

Höland, A (1998), Rechtfertigungsdruck, *Mitbestimmung*, vol. 44, no. 6, pp. 64-67.

Hoffmann, R. (1997a), Europäische Betriebsräte - ein Baustein zur Europäisierung industrieller Beziehungen, in: J. Deppe et. al. (eds.), *Europäische Betriebsräte Wege in ein soziales Europa*, Frankfurt/New York, pp. 115-30.

Hoffmann, R. (1997b), Über die nationalen Grenzen hinaus, *Die Quelle*, vol. 48, p. 6 f.

Hyman, R. (1996), Die Geometrie des Gewerkschaftsverhaltens: Eine vergleichende Analyse von Identitäten und Ideologien, in: *Industrielle Beziehungen*, vol. 3, no. 1, pp. 5-35.

IG Metall (1999), *Elektrohausgeräte - Branchenanalyse*, Frankfurt am Main, Juli 1999.

Internationaler Metallgewerkschaftsbund: *ELECTROLUX - Das Spiel mit der Globalstrategie*.

Internationaler Metallgewerkschaftsbund: *ELECTROLUX - Die Herausforderungen der Neunziger Jahre*.

Jachtenfuchs, M. and Kohler-Koch, B. (1996), Einleitung: Regieren im dynamischen Mehr-Ebenensystem, in: M. Jachtenfuchs and B. Kohler Koch (eds.), *Europäische Integration*, Opladen, pp. 15-44.

Jacobi, O. (1997), Stichtag 1.1.99, in: *Mitbestimmung*, vol. 43, no. 7 and 8, pp. 54-7.

Jacobi, O. (1998), Europäische Kollektivvereinbarungen - Vision oder Illusion?, in: *Gewerkschaftliche Monatshefte*, vol. 49, no. 6 and 7.

Jaeger, R. (1996), Euro-Betriebsräte und Entwicklung transnationaler Kommunikationsstrukturen - Praxis und Perspektiven, in: *WSI- Mitteilungen*, vol. 49, no. 8, pp. 483-88.

Jaeger, R. (1998), Europäische Aktiengesellschaft - was ist das schon wieder?, in: *Der Betriebsrat*, no. 1, p. 5-10.

Kasten, G. and Soskice, D. (1999), Tarifverhandlungen in "Euroland", in: *WZB-Mitteilungen* vol. 83, March 1999, pp. 21-23.

Keller, B. (1999), Supranationale Regulierung von Arbeitsverhältnissen - Das Beispiel der EU, *WSI Mitteilungen*, vol. 52, no. 2, pp. 109-18.

Kohler-Koch, B. (1996), Die Gestaltungsmacht organisierter Interessen, in M. Jachtenfuchs, B. Kohler-Koch (eds.), *Europäische Integration*, Opladen, pp. 193-222.

Koubeck, N., Cleff, Th., Pierotti, Ch., and Schafmeister, S. (1996), *Unter nehmensstrategien in der Triade*, Baden-Baden.

Krieger, H., Fröhlich, D. (1998), Gibt es bei den neuen Formen der Arbeitsorganisation in Deutschland eine Modernisierungslücke? - Die Praxis direkter Arbeitnehmerbeteiligung in Europa und den USA, *WSI- Mitteilungen*, vol. 51, no. 3, pp. 153-64.

Lane, Ch. (1994), Industrial Order and the Transformation of Industrial Relations: Britain, Germany and France compared, in R. Hyman and A. Ferner (eds.): *New Frontiers in European Industrial Relations*, Oxford, pp. 167-95.

Lawerino, R. (1997), *Demokratische Partizipation in der Chemischen Industrie der Bundesrepublik Deutschland - Final report*.

Lecher, W. (1994), Euro-Betriebsräte: Ein empirisch gestützter deutschfranzösischer Vergleich, *WSI-Mitteilungen*, vol. 47, no. 2, pp. 108-16.

Lecher, W. (1994), Betriebliche Funktionsfähigkeit der französischen und deutschen Arbeitnehmerinteressenvertretung - ein empirisch gestützter Vergleich, in: *Industrielle Beziehungen*, vol. 1, no. 2, pp. 179-202.

Lecher, W. (1997), *Gewerkschaften und industrielle Beziehungen in Frankreich, Italien, Großbritannien und Deutschland - Rahmenbedingungen für die EBR*, WSI-Diskussionspapier No. 30, Düsseldorf, January.

Lecher, W. (1998), Mitbestimmung durch Tarifpolitik - ein europäisches Thema? in: *Gewerkschaftliche Monatshefte*, vol. 49, no. 10, pp. 679-85.

Lecher, W. (ed.) (1998), *Europäische Betriebsräte und Arbeitsbeziehungen - zur Lage und Entwicklung in Großbritannien, Frankreich und Italien*, Graue Reihe der HBS, Düsseldorf.

Lecher, W. (1999), Europäisierung der Tarifpolitik – Eine Chance?, in: H.G. Nutzinger (ed.): *Perspektiven der Mitbestimmung*, Marburg, pp. 335-46.

Lecher, W. and Platzer, H.-W. (1996), Europäische Betriebsräte: Fundament und Instrument europäischer Arbeitsbeziehungen? - Probleme der Kompatibilität von nationalen Arbeitnehmervertretungen und EBR, in: WSI-Mitte*ilungen*, vol. 49, no. 8, pp. 503-12.

Lecher, W., Nagel, B. and Platzer, H.-W. (1998), *Die Konstituierung EuropäischerBetriebsräte vom Informationsausschuß zum Akteur?*, Baden-Baden.

Leonardi, S. (1997), Partecipazione: note critiche sul modello Zanussi, in: *Lavoro Informazione*, no. 14, pp. 13-26.

Marginson, P. and Sisson, K. (1998), European Collective Bargaining: a Virtual Prospect?, in: *Journal of Common Market Studies*, vol. 4, no. 36, pp. 505-28.

Mertens, H. (1994), *Europaweite Kooperation von Betriebsräten multina tionaler Konzerne - Das Beispiel des VW-Konzerns*

Minghini, C. (1996), Una marcia troppo lenta. In: *Rassegna Sindacale*, 40, 19.11.1996.

Mondini, M. (1999), Beitrag beim "Europäischen Gespräch 1998: Die Zukunft der Mitbestimmung in Europa", *Die Mitbestimmung*, No. 3, supplement, pp. VI-VII.

Müller, W. (1998), *Betriebsräte zur Wallstreet? - Einflußnahme auf die Konzernpolitik von multinationalen Konzernen per "shareholder democracy?*, Hans-Böckler-Stiftung, Düsseldorf.

Müller-Jentsch, W. (1995), Auf dem Prüfstand: Das deutsche Modell der industriellen Beziehungen, in: *Industrielle Beziehungen*, vol. 2, no. 1, pp. 11-24.

Müller-Jentsch, W (1996), Theorien Industrieller Beziehungen, *Industrielle Beziehungen*, vol. 3, no. 1, pp. 36-64.

Müller-Jentsch, W., Sperling, H.-J. and Weyrather, I. (1997), *Neue Technologien in der Verhandlungsarena - Schweden, Großbritannien und Deutschland im Vergleich, Schriftenreihe Industrielle Beziehungen*.

Nagel, B., Riess, B., Rüb, St. and Beschorner, A. (1996), *Information und Mitbestimmung im internationalen Konzern*, Baden-Baden.

Namuth, M. (1999), Permanentes Experiment, in: *Die Mitbestimmung*, vol. 45, no. 5, pp. 51-53.

Niedenhoff, H.-U. (1997), *Der Europäische Betriebsrat - Gesetz, Kritik und Beispiele erster Konstruktionen; Kölner Texte und Thesen*, Köln.

Platzer, H.-W. (1991), *Gewerkschaftspolitik ohne Grenzen?*, Bonn.

Platzer, H.-W. (1999), Die EU – Sozial - und Beschäftigungspolitik nach Amsterdam: Koordinierte und verhandelte Europäisierung, in: *Integration*, vol. 22, no. 3, pp. 176-98.

Platzer, H.-W. and Weiner. K.-P. (1998), Europäische Betriebsräte – eine Konstituionsanalyse, Zur Genese und Dynamik transnationaler Arbeitsbeziehungen, *Industrielle Beziehungen*, vol. 5, no. 4, pp. 388-412.

Projekt Euro-Betriebsräte bei der IG Metall (Ed.) (1997), *Handbuch für europäische Betriebsräte, 2nd. revision, August*, Frankfurt/Main.

Rath, F. (1991), Strukturelle Koordinaten gewerkschaftlicher Europapolitik, in: W. Däubler and W. Lecher (eds.) *Die Gewerkschaften in den 12 EG-Ländern*, Köln, pp. 233-83.

Saba, L. (1992), Le prospettive del modello partecipativo, in: *Il Progetto*, vol. 70, pp. 71-82.

Sack, B. (1998), Erfahrungsbericht über den Europäischen Betriebsrat bei Kraft-Jacobs-Suchard, in W. Eberwein and J. Tholen (eds.), *Euro-Betriebsräte und deutsche Betriebsverfassung*, Bremen, pp. 55-59.

Sateriale, G. (1998), Anche la partecipazione Zanussi alla dell'Europa, in: *L'impresa al plurale. Quaderni della partecipazione*, no. 2, pp. 391-99.

Scharpf, F. W. (1996), Politische Optionen im vollendeten Binnenmarkt, M. Jachtenfuchs and B. Kohler-Koch (eds.), *Europäische Integration*, Opladen, pp. 109-40.

Schmid, K.-P. (1999), Flucht aus dem Tarif, in: *Die ZEIT*, No. 20, 12th of May, 1999, p. 32.

Schmidt, E. (1997), *Beteiligung an betrieblichen Umweltschutzmaßnahmen (insbesondere Öko-Audits) als Gestaltungsaufgabe für europäische Betriebsräte in der chemischen Industrie, Hans-Böckler-Stiftung, Final report*, Düsseldorf.

Schmierl. K. (1998), Amorphie im "Normierten Verhandlungssystem" - Wandel industrieller Beziehungen im internationalen Unternehmensverbund, in: M. von Behr and H. Hirsch-Kreinsen (eds.), *Globale Produktion und Industriearbeit*, Frankfurt/New York, pp. 145-177.

Schulten, Th. (1998), Tarifpolitik unter den Bedingungen der Europäischen Währungsunion, in: *WSI-Mitteilungen*, vol. 51, no. 7, pp. 482-93.

Schulten, Th. (1999), Arbeitsbeziehungen im Euroland – Chancen und Widerstände einer Europäisierung der Tarifpolitik, in: *SPW*, Heft 105, no. 1, pp. 33-6.

Schulten, Th. and Bispinck, R. (eds.) (1999), *Tarifpolitik unter dem Euro - Perspektiven einer europäischen Koordinierung: das Beispiel Metallindustrie*, Hamburg.

Schuster, J. (1998), *Europäische Beschäftigungspolitik – Beschäftigungsförderung und Mehrebenenregulation*, Dortmund.

Spiegel, Der (1999), No. 14, Hamburg.

Streeck, W. (1998), Gewerkschaften zwischen Nationalstaat und Europäischer Union, *WSI-Mitteilungen*, vol. 51, no. 1, pp. 1-14.

Streeck, W. and Vitols, S. (1993), *European Works Councils: Between statutory Enactment and Voluntary Adoption, WZB, discussion paper*, Berlin.

Stützel, W. (1996), Euro-Betriebsräte - Verrechtlichung erzwingt Handeln, in: *Industrielle Beziehungen*, vol. 3, no. 3, pp. 278-86.

Traxler, F. (1996), European Trade Union Policy and Collective Bargaining: Mechanisms and Levels of Labour Market Regulation in Comparison, in: *Transfer*, vol. 2, no. 2, pp. 287-97.

Volz, R. (1997), Konvergenz und Divergenz von Arbeitsbeziehungen in multinationalen Unternehmen - Die Nahrungsmittelindustrie und der Bankensektor im Drei-Länder-Vergleich, in: *Industrielle Beziehungen*, vol. 4, no. 2, pp. 79-100.

Voswinkel, St., Lücking, St. and Bode, I. (1996), *Im Schatten des Fordismus - Industrielle Beziehungen in der Bauwirtschaft und im Gastgewerbe Deutschlands und Frankreichs, Schriftenreihe Industrielle Beziehungen*, München u. Mering.

Waddington, J., Hoffmann, R. and Lind, J. (1997), European trade unionism in transition? a review of the issues, in: *Transfer*, vol. 3, no. 3, pp. 464-85.

Wagner, E., Rehmert, Ch. and Schmidt, M. (1996), *Interkulturelle Kommunikation und Kooperation in Europa, Final report*, University Hildesheim.

Ziltener, P. (1999), *Strukturwandel der europäischen Integration - Die Europäische Union und die Veränderung von Staatlichkeit*, Münster.

Index

ABC company
  EWC
    case study 119-32
    establishment 122-4
    and national interests 129-30
    reforms 126-8
    role 129-32
    structure 124
    working methods 124-5
  structure 120-2
AEEU (Amalgamated Engineering Electrical Union)
  and collective bargaining 69
  on the EMF 62
  and Eurofederations 61
  and Europeanisation 57
  and EWCs 46
Alusuisse Lonza Group AG 89-90
  culture 86
  EWC
    cultural problems 92-3
    establishment 88-9
    language problems 92
    management view of 93-4
    participants' view of 94-6
    role in VIAG merger 84, 96-100
    structure 89-90
    training 93
    working methods 90-2
  organisation 85
  turnover 86
  VIAG merger
    case study 84-100
    failure 88, 98-9
    problems 87-8
    rationale 87

Astra company, Zeneca company, merger 142-4
AstraZeneca company
  EWC
    case study 140-56
    matters discussed 151-2
    participants' view of 152-3
    problems 154-5
    structure 151
  see also Zeneca company

CFDT (Democratic Worker's Confederation) 58
CGT (General Confederation of Work) 58
CGT-FO (General Confederation of Labour-Workers Power) 58
chemicals industry
  European trade union co-operation 48-9
  and Europeanisation 58
co-determination
  and European company framework 49-52, 54
  and Italy 52
  and UK 52
COBAS (basis committees), Italy 11
collective bargaining
  and the AEEU 69
  construction industry 34-5
  and the EFBWW 70
  and the EMF 70
  and the Euro 64-5
  and Eurofederations 72
  Europe 34-5
    introduction 68-9
  Europeanisation of 64-8, 74-80,

161-2
  co-ordination 70
  criticism 69-70
  suitable areas 71-3
and EWCs 79
France 9, 69-70
Germany
  employers' associations 68, 72
  trade unions 67, 69, 71-2
and the GMB 69
and IG Metall 65-6
Italy 11
and Social Dialogue 74-5, 76, 162
and the TGWU 69
trade unions
  Italy 72
  UK 69
UK 8
  employers' associations 68
and UNICE 73
and UNIFI 69
see also pay bargaining
companies, and Europeanisation 40, 54
company
  European
    and co-determination 49-52, 54
    Germany 50-1
    and IG Metall 50-1
    legal framework for 49-50
construction industry
  collective bargaining 34-5
  and internationalisation 40

Danone company, and EWCs 30
Davignon group 50
DEC (Digital Equipment Corporation), and EWCs 29-30
deregulation
  world economy 20
  see also globalisation

EEF (Engineering Employers' Federation), and EWCs 47

EFBWW (European Federation of Building and Woodworkers) 35
  and collective bargaining 70
  and Eurofederations 61
EIRO (European Industrial Relations Observatory) 67
Electrolux-Zanussi company
  employees 102
  EWC
    role in restructuring 101, 109-19
    structure 108-9
  restructuring
    case study 101-19
    proposals 107-8
  structure 102-3
  see also Zanussi company
EMF (European Metalworkers Federation)
  AEEU on 62
  and collective bargaining 70
  and Eurofederations 61
  TGWU on 62
employers
  Britain, Europeanisation 59
  and EWCs 28, 31, 33, 47, 52, 55-6
  Germany, and Europeanisation 58
  trade unions, alliances 41
employers' associations
  Europe, collective bargaining 72-3
  Germany 63
    collective bargaining 68, 72
  information exchange 68
  role 62-3
  structure 62
  and subsidiarity 79
  UK, collective bargaining 68
  weakness 66
EMU (European Monetary Union)
  and economic integration 16
  and industrial relations 1, 16-17
ETUC (European Trade Union Confederation) 67-8
  and Social Dialogue 76

ETUI (European Trade Union Institute) 68
Euro currency, and collective bargaining 64-5
Eurofederations
  and the AEEU 61
  co-operation with national trade unions 60-1, 163-4
  and collective bargaining 72
  criticism of 61-2
  and the EFBWW 61
  and EMF 61
  and EWCs 32, 33, 47-8, 60-1
  and French trade unions 62
  and German trade unions 61
  and the GMB 61
  and GPMU 61
  and subsidiarity 78
  and the TGWU 61
  and UCATT 61
  and UK trade unions 61-2
  and UNIFI 61
Europe
  collective bargaining 34-5
  industrial relations
    comparison 12
    theory 22-3
  integration 13, 14-16
  wages, convergence 66
European Central Bank 64-5
European Commission, and subsidiarity 78-9
European trade union co-operation, chemicals industry 48-9
European Trade Union Confederation 66, 67
European trade union federations *see* Eurofederations
Europeanisation
  and the AEEU 57
  and chemicals industry 58
  collective bargaining 64-8, 74-80, 161-2
  and companies 40, 54
  employers, UK 58, 59
  and EWCs 158-9

Germany 40
  and the GMB 57
  and IG BCE 57
  impetus for 39
  and industrial relations 40, 54, 77-9, 159-61, 164-5
  meaning 17
  and the metal industry 58
  nature of 157-8
  of pay bargaining 35
  and Social Dialogue 73
  and socio-political integration 17-18, 37
  and the TGWU 57
  trade unions 54-5, 55, 158
    France 58
    Germany 57, 77-8
    Italy 57
    UK 57-8
  and the TUC 57-8
  UK 40
  and UNICE 59-60
  and the WEM 59
EWC (European Works Councils)
  ABC company
    case study 119-32
    establishment 122-4
    and national interests 129-30
    reforms 126-8
    role 129-32
    structure 124
    working methods 124-5
  advantages 41-2
  and the AEEU 46
  Alusuisse Lonza Group AG
    cultural problems 92-3
    establishment 88-9
    language problems 92
    management view of 93-4
    participants' view of 94-6
    role in VIAG merger 84, 96-100
    structure 89-90
    training AG 93
    working methods 90-2
  AstraZeneca company

case study 140-56
matters discussed 151-2
participants' view of 152-3
problems 154-5
structure 151
and collective bargaining 79
and Danone company 30
and DEC company 29-30
demand for 24-5
Directive, revision 44-5
disadvantages 42
and the EEF 47
Electrolux-Zanussi company
  role in restructuring 101, 109-19
  structure 108-9
employers' attitude 28, 31, 33, 47, 52
establishment 1
and European trade union federations 32, 33, 47-8, 60-1
and Europeanisation 158-9
France 42, 46, 48
Germany 29, 33, 42, 43, 46
and the GMB 43
and IG Metall 45, 57
and industrial relations, national 53
influence 26, 28
and information flow 30, 31
Italy 43, 46, 48
and job security 30
Kafer Isoliertechnik company
  case study 132-40
  establishment 134
  participants' view of 136-7
  problems 135
  role 136, 139-40
  and trade unions 137-8
and language problems 32, 33
legal rights 31
and national law 28-9
numbers 53
in practice 43-4
problems 28-30, 38, 53
role 31

and Social Dialogue 74
success factors 155-6
and the TGWU 46
threshold establishment 45-6
and trade unions 28, 32, 33, 42-3, 44, 45, 52
and the UCATT 43
UK 42, 43, 44, 46
and UNICE 44, 47
and VW 29
and the WEM 45
Zeneca company
  establishment 144
  matters discussed 147-50
  structure 144-5
  working methods 146-7

FIEC (Federation of the European Construction Industry) 66
FIET (International Association of White Collar Employees) 68
  and Social Dialogue 76
food industry, Social Dialogue 77
France
  collective bargaining 9, 69-70
  EWCs 42, 46, 48
  Germany, industrial relations, compared 10
  industrial relations 8-10
  and Social Dialogue 75
  trade unions
    and Eurofederations 62
    Europeanisation 58

Germany
  employers' associations 63
    collective bargaining 68, 72
    and Europeanisation 58
  and European company framework 50-1
  Europeanisation 40
  EWCs 29, 33, 42, 43, 46
  France, industrial relations, compared 10
  industrial relations 6-7, 36-7
  and Social Dialogue 75, 76-7

trade unions 4, 7, 57
   collective bargaining 67, 69, 71-2
   and Eurofederations 61
   Europeanisation 57, 77-8
   UK, industrial relations, compared 7-8
   worker representation 36-7
   Works councils 7
globalisation
   and industrial relations 20
   meaning 20 n.1
   see also deregulation; internationalisation
GMB (General Workers' Union)
   and collective bargaining 69
   and ECWs 43
   and Eurofederations 61
   Europeanisation 57
GPMU (Graphical, Paper & Media Union), and Eurofederations 61

IG BCE (Industrial Union for the Mining, the Chemicals Industry & Energy), Europeanisation 57
IG Metall
   and collective bargaining 65-6
   and European companies 50-1
   and EWCs 45, 57
industrial relations
   and EMU 1, 16-17
   Europe, comparison 12
   Europeanisation 40, 54-5, 77-9, 159-61, 164-5
   France 8-10
   Germany 6-7, 36-7
   and globalisation 20
   Italy 10-11, 41
   meaning 2
   national, and EWCs 53
   national variations 27
   and production processes 20-1
   theories 18-19
   Zanussi company 104-7
information, and EWCs 30, 31
insurance industry,
   internationalisation 40
integration
   economic, and EMU 16
   socio-political, and Europeanisation 17-18
internationalisation
   and construction industry 40
   insurance industry 40
   production processes 25
   see also globalisation
Italy
   and co-determination 52
   COBAS 11
   collective bargaining 11
   EWCs 43, 46, 48
   industrial relations 10-11, 41
   and Social Dialogue 76
   trade unions
      collective bargaining 72
      Europeanisation 57
   worker representation 37

job security, and EWCs 30

Kafer Isoliertechnik company
   EWC
      case study 132-40
      establishment 134
      participants' view of 136-7
      problems 135
      role 136, 139-40
      and trade unions 137-8
   restructuring 133, 138-9
   structure 132-3
   workforce reduction 133-4

language problems, and EWCs 32, 33

Maastricht, Treaty of 24, 73
metal industry
   and Europeanisation 58
   Social Dialogue 77

pay bargaining
   Europeanisation of 35

see also collective bargaining
production processes
  changes 21
  fordist 21
  and industrial relations 20-1
  internationalisation 25
  and trade unions 21-2

SE (European Public Company), framework for creating 49-50
shop stewards, UK 7
Social Dialogue
  and collective bargaining 74-5, 76, 162
  and the ETUC 76
  and Europeanisation 73
  and EWCs 74
  and FIET 76
  food industry 77
  forms of 73-4
  and France 75
  and Germany 75, 76-7
  and Italy 76
  metal industry 77
  role 75-7
  and UK 75-6
  and UNICE 74-5
subsidiarity
  and employers' associations 79
  and Eurofederations 78
  and the European Commission 78-9

TGWU (Transport and General Workers' Union)
  and collective bargaining 69
  on the EMF 62
  and Eurofederations 61
  and Europeanisation 57
  and EWCs 46
trade unions
  employers, alliances 41
  and Europeanisation 54-5, 55, 158
  and EWCs 28, 32, 33, 42-3, 44, 45, 52

France
  and Eurofederations 62
  Europeanisation 58
Germany 4, 7
  collective bargaining 67, 69, 71-2
  Europeanisation 57, 77-8
Italy
  collective bargaining 72
  Europeanisation 57
national, co-operation with European trade union federations 60-1, 163-4
and production processes 21-2
UK
  collective bargaining 69
  Europeanisation 57-8
TUC (Trades Union Congress), and Europeanisation 57-8

UCATT (Union of Construction Allied Trades and Technicians)
  and Eurofederations 61
  and EWCs 43
UK
  and co-determination 52
  collective bargaining 8
  employers' associations 68
  employers, Europeanisation 59
  Europeanisation 40
  EWCs 42, 43, 44, 46
  Germany, industrial relations, compared 7-8
  shop stewards 7-8
  and Social Dialogue 75-6
  trade unions
    collective bargaining 69
    and Eurofederations 61-2
    Europeanisation 57-8
  worker representation 37
UNICE (Union of Industrial and Employer Associations of Europe)
  and collective bargaining 73
  and Europeanisation 59-60
  and EWCs 44, 47
  role 62, 63

and Social Dialogue 74-5
UNIFI (Finance Industry Union)
and collective bargaining 69
and Eurofederations 61

VIAG, merger with Alusuisse Lonza
Group AG, case study 84-100
VW (Volkswagen)
and EWCs 29
worker representation 26
wages, Europe, convergence 66
WEM (Western European Metal
Trade Employers Organisation)
and Europeanisation 59
and EWCs 45
worker representation
Germany 36-7
Italy 37
UK 37

VW 26
Works councils, Germany 7

Zanussi company
industrial relations 104-7
products 104
structure 103-4
see also Electrolux-Zanussi
company
Zeneca company
Astra company, merger 142-4
EWC
establishment 144
matters discussed 147-50
structure 144-5
working methods 146-7
structure 141
workforce 141
see also AstraZeneca company